Acclaim for **YOU CAN COUNT ON ME**

"Richly rewarding."   —*Houston Chronicle*

"A delicately drawn drama that explores the ties that bind two adult siblings . . . full of hope and humor."   —*People*

"Generous and honest."   —*US Weekly*

"One of [*You Can Count on Me*]'s major strengths is in the way it examines the ordinary. From such simplicity comes greatness."
—*St. Louis Dispatch*

"A subtle and often surprising study of the relationship between damaged adult siblings, full of mordant humor and dramatic invention. Lonergan has a terrific ear for dialogue and understands that people don't shift course once or twice in a lifetime but virtually every day, sometimes in the middle of a conversation."
—Salon.com

"Who'd have thought so much of the universe could be crammed into Scottsville, N.Y.; who knew so much life thrived, hummed, buzzed, and throbbed just off the interstate?"
—*The Washington Post*

Kenneth Lonergan

YOU CAN COUNT ON ME

Kenneth Lonergan is a screenwriter and playwright whose works include the original screenplay for *Analyze This* and *The Lost Army,* and the plays *Lobby Hero, The Waverly Gallery,* and *This Is Our Youth. You Can Count on Me* marked his feature film directorial debut. The film was nominated for two Academy Awards and was awarded Best Screenplay at the Sundance Film Festival, among other numerous awards. He lives in New York City with his wife, actress J. Smith-Cameron.

Also by Kenneth Lonergan

PLAYS

Lobby Hero
The Waverly Gallery
This Is Our Youth

YOU CAN COUNT ON ME

YOU CAN COUNT ON ME
A Screenplay

Kenneth Lonergan

VINTAGE BOOKS
A Division of Random House, Inc.
New York

Library of Congress Cataloging-in-Publication Data

Lonergan, Kenneth.
    You can count on me : a screenplay / by Kenneth Lonergan.
       p.   cm.
    ISBN 0-375-71392-1
    I. You can count on me (Motion picture)   II. Title.
  PN1997 .Y52 2001
791.43'72—dc21   2001046773

Book design by Fritz Metsch

www.vintagebooks.com

Printed in the United States of America

10 9 8 7 6 5 4 3 2 1

INTRODUCTION

Screenplays are not usually read just for fun the way you read a novel or even a play. For one thing, so much of a movie is conveyed by the acting, camera, lighting, editing, sound editing and music that compared to the finished film the screenplay always seems a bit flat and colorless. For another, the screenplay of a finished film will never again be brought to life the way the text of a play will be. Movies do get remade occasionally, of course, but generally speaking, the better the original film, the less point there always seems to be in remaking it. In the theater the exact opposite is true: The better the play, the more general the interest there is in seeing it produced again over time.

That's why, I imagine most people read screenplays for professional reasons, or because they are curious about the origins of a movie they've already seen. Sometimes it is a very general guideline, frequently departed from and just as frequently ignored during shooting, rewritten daily, improvised on, and so forth; and sometimes, as in this case, it is very faithfully followed, the way you would follow the text of a play you were rehearsing. This is rarer, obviously, even for directors who write their own movies. The script for *You Can Count on Me* was followed very closely because I didn't really know any other way to work. As such, it may be fun reading for admirers of the film who want to see for themselves the difference between a written and an acted scene; to see what colors and characteristics were brought into the movies by the actors, cinematographer, editor, etc. For people who like the movie it's probably hard to disassociate the written characters from the excellent and subtle performances by Laura Linney, Mark Ruffalo, Rory Culkin, Matthew Broderick, Jon Tenney and the rest of the cast; but of course there's no real need to. One can also hope the story is interesting to read in and of itself, even in its original form.

Kenneth Lonergan
New York, October 2001

YOU CAN COUNT ON ME

FADE IN: INT./EXT. A CAR (MOVING). NIGHT.

The shifting lights from the odd passing car play over the faces of MR. *and* MRS. PRESCOTT, *a pleasant-looking couple in their late thirties, dressed up for a night out. Mr. Prescott drives them along a dark hilly two-lane highway.*

> MRS. PRESCOTT
> Why do they always put braces on teenage girls at the *exact* moment when they're the most self-conscious about their appearance?

Pause.

> MR. PRESCOTT
> I don't know.

UP AHEAD, *near the top of the oncoming hill, a* RED PICKUP TRUCK *is poking its nose out of the short exit lane.*

> MRS. PRESCOTT
> Tom—

> MR. PRESCOTT
> I see him . . .

The PICKUP LURCHES *into the road, with not nearly enough time to spare.*

MRS. PRESCOTT	MR. PRESCOTT
Tom!	Jesus!

Mr. Prescott swerves OVER *the* DOUBLE SOLID WHITE LINE *and clears the truck as—*

Another pair of HEADLIGHTS *from an oncoming truck* RISES UP *over the* HILL *directly in* FRONT *of them—*

MRS. PRESCOTT (Screams)

Tom!

Mr. Prescott's FOOT STOMPS *on the* BRAKE. *We* BLACK OUT *and there is the* SOUND *of a terrible* CRASH.

CUT TO:

EXT. THE PRESCOTTS' FRONT DOOR. NIGHT.

The SHADOW *of a big man looms up onto the front door. A big finger* RINGS *the* BELL.

A moment.

AMY, *a thirteen-year-old baby-sitter with braces, opens the door and looks up. In the b.g. we see* TWO CHILDREN, SAMMY *(Samantha) and* TERRY PRESCOTT, *in their pajamas, lying on their stomachs in the living room, watching television. Sammy is eleven. Terry is eight.*

REVERSE: DARRYL, *the* SHERIFF, *a portly fellow with glasses and a mustache, looks down at* AMY.

SHERIFF

Hello, Amy.

AMY (Puzzled)

Hi, Darryl.

SHERIFF (Thinking)

Amy, would you please tell the kids you'll be right back, and then shut the door and come outside to talk to us for a minute?

AMY

OK. *(To kids)* Be right back, you guys!

SAMMY

You're not supposed to go out, Amy.

TERRY

She's going to smoke a cigarette.

AMY *closes the door and looks expectantly up at Darryl. Darryl doesn't know how to start.*

EXT. CHURCH. DAY.

CREDITS BEGIN OVER *a blustery April day. The steeple of the little white church stands out against the sharp blue sky.*

INT. TOWN CHURCH. DAY.

It's a small church and a small congregation, but it's full. There's a CHOIR *of mostly* SENIOR CITIZENS *arrayed in the back.* TWO CLOSED CASKETS *are laid out in front of the* MINISTER, *a fiftyish woman with thick glasses and salt-and-pepper hair, who is giving a eulogy* MOS.

Among the mourners in the second row sit Terry and Sammy, both red-eyed, and uncomfortable in their dress-up clothes. Their Aunt Ruth, a pinch-faced woman in her forties, sits next to them.

Sammy and Terry are holding hands tightly. Terry wipes his eyes with his free hand.

The Minister addresses her remarks to the children. Sammy is hanging on the Minister's every word; Terry is shifting his eyes and his seat as if it will kill him to sit still another minute.

DISSOLVE TO:

EXT. SCOTTSVILLE CEMETERY. SIXTEEN YEARS LATER. DAY.

On the beautiful hill overlooking the beautiful windy green country, SAMMY, *twenty-seven years old now, puts flowers on her parents' graves with quick, practiced movements.*

She is a nice-looking young woman of a neat appearance, saved from primness by an elusive, pleasantly flustered quality. An unsuccessfully neat person. She is dressed in office clothes—white blouse, dark skirt, high heels, light raincoat over everything. She picks out a couple of weeds and then bows her head and closes her eyes.

CREDITS END.

EXT. SCOTTSVILLE—MAIN STREET. DAY.

Scottsville is a small town. Main Street. Run-down old stores next to a new bank, a couple of chain stores, a few restaurants of varying ambitions. Civil War statue. World War I statue. World War II statue. Residential streets wandering away from Main Street up and down hills. You know there's a minimall somewhere nearby. A fair amount of activity during the daytime.

SAMMY'S CAR *pulls up across the street from where an eight-year-old* BOY *in a secondhand baseball jacket and a school knapsack is waiting at the curb. This is her son,* RUDY. SAMMY *calls out the car window.*

> SAMMY
> Rudy, come on! I'm really late!

Rudy hurries across the street and gets in the car, slinging his knapsack into the backseat.

INT. THE CAR (MOVING). DAY.

> SAMMY
> How was school?

> RUDY
> Stupid.

> SAMMY
> Why do you say that?

> RUDY
> We're supposed to write a story for English homework, but they didn't tell us what it's supposed to be about.

> SAMMY
> What do you mean?

> RUDY
> I mean they didn't tell us what it's supposed to *be* about. They said do whatever you want.

> SAMMY
> So what's wrong with that?

> RUDY
> Nothing. I just think it's unstructured.

SAMMY *(Smiles)*
Well, I'm sure you'll be able to think of something. If you can't, I'll help you.

INT./EXT. CAR/CAROL'S HOUSE. DAY.

Sammy stops the car outside a heavily THICKETED DRIVEWAY (CAROL'S HOUSE), *and* RUDY *gets out.*

SAMMY
Don't forget your backpack.

Rudy returns to take his knapsack out of the back.

RUDY
It's not a backpack, it's a knapsack.

SAMMY
Don't forget your knapsack.

Rudy hoists his knapsack out of the back.

SAMMY
Give me a kiss.

Rudy gives her a kiss and puts his arms around her and squeezes her neck.

He withdraws, slams the door. As Sammy DRIVES AWAY, *he slogs up the long twisting driveway.*

EXT. MERCHANTS NATIONAL TRUST—PARKING LOT. DAY.

Sammy gets out of her car, which is parked in one of the half dozen spaces in the little parking lot allocated for bank employees.

She hurries toward the employees' entrance, fixing her skirt as she goes.

INT. MERCHANTS NATIONAL TRUST. DAY.

Sammy hurries down the clean hallway in the back past MABEL, *a pleasant-faced fellow employee.*

> MABEL
> Guess who's been asking for you?

> SAMMY
> Oh no, really?

Mabel nods and passes by.

SAMMY KNOCKS *on a big door that says "Manager" and has half the letters of the previous branch manager's name taken off it.*

> BRIAN *(Inside)*
> Yeah, come in!

Sammy swings open the door. BRIAN EVERETT, *the new branch manager, is unpacking a box. Sammy is surprised to see he is in his early thirties and very good-looking in a boyish sort of way; he wears shirt-sleeves and tie, and a wedding ring.*

> SAMMY
> Mr. Everett?

> BRIAN
> Yeah: Brian.

> SAMMY
> Brian. Hi. I'm Samantha Prescott—I'm the lending officer?

> BRIAN
> Yeah, hi, how are you? Come on in. Sit down.

Sammy comes into the office and sits.

> SAMMY
>
> I am so sorry I was late . . .

> BRIAN
>
> Yeah, we missed you before . . .

> SAMMY
>
> I got held up. Believe me, it is not something I make a habit of . . .

> BRIAN
>
> I'm sure it's not. Actually—could you just, could you close that door for me? Thanks.

Sammy gets up and closes the door.

INT. BRIAN'S OFFICE. LATER.

Sammy sits in front of Brian's desk. Brian is behind the desk listening.

> SAMMY
>
> —so I always just run out at 3:15 to pick him up and then run him real quick over to the sitter's house. Anyway, Larry never minded about it and I was just hoping it would be OK with you too . . .

> BRIAN
>
> Well—Samantha—I realize that Scottsville is not exactly a major banking center . . .

> SAMMY
>
> No it's not . . .

> BRIAN
>
> No—I know it's not. . . . But it's kind of a personal challenge to me to see what we can do to bring local service up to the same kinds of standards we'd be trying to meet if we *were* the biggest branch in the state. And that means I don't want *anybody* running out at 3:15 or 3:30, or whenever the bus happens to come in that day.

Now is there anybody else who can pick your son up after school? Does your husband work in the area? Do you—

SAMMY

Oh—No—Rudy Sr. isn't "on the scene." So to speak.

BRIAN

Well, I can give you a couple of days to make some other arrangement, but . . .

SAMMY

Well—Brian? I understand what you're saying, and I think it's great. I do. Because there's a lot of things around here that could use some attention. Believe me. But I've honestly been meeting that bus every day for four years now and it really does take just fifteen minutes, and if I take the time out of my lunch hour . . .

BRIAN

I'd really prefer it if you would make some other arrangement. OK?

SAMMY *(Brightly)*

I'll do my best . . . !

Brian kicks back in his chair and puts his hands behind his head.

BRIAN

How old's your son?

SAMMY

He's eight.

BRIAN

That's a terrific age.

INT. SAMMY'S CAR (MOVING). DUSK.

Sammy and Rudy drive home in silence. The orange sunlight flickers through the trees and onto their faces as they drive along.

EXT. PRESCOTT (SAMMY'S) HOUSE. DUSK.

The same house that Sammy grew up in, with sixteen years' more wear on it.

Sammy's car swings expertly by the mailbox, and Rudy reaches half his body out of the passenger window and gets the mail.

INT. SAMMY'S HOUSE. DUSK.

Sammy comes into the house carrying two bags of groceries. Rudy follows, looking through the mail. Sammy passes through the house and goes into the kitchen.

RUDY

You got a letter from Uncle Terry.

SAMMY

What?!

Her whole face lights up and she grabs the letter. She tears it open and reads it with growing excitement.

INT. SAMMY'S BEDROOM. LATER.

Sammy opens her FILE DRAWER. *Inside are tax files, household files, miscellaneous files.*

She puts Terry's letter away in a very full file marked **"Terry— Correspondence."** *The folder is stuffed with other letters, on all different kinds of stationery from all over the country, all from Terry.*

INT. DINING ROOM. NIGHT.

Sammy and Rudy are eating dinner. It's a biggish house for just two people.

RUDY

Whose room is he gonna stay in?

SAMMY

He can stay in the little room. *(Pause)* But you know what? He's not going to live here. He's only gonna stay for a little while. . . . And it's OK if you don't remember him, because you were only six the last time he was here. . . . But it'll be nice if you got a chance to get to know each other a little bit. Don't you think?

Rudy looks worried and doesn't answer.

INT. LIVING ROOM. LATER.

Rudy is on the floor, writing in his school composition notebook. Sammy comes downstairs.

>   SAMMY
> Rudy? Would it distract you if I put on some music?

>   RUDY
> No.

She puts on a CD, *sits down and picks up a book. She looks at Rudy, who is writing away.*

>   SAMMY
> Did you think of a story?

>   RUDY
> Uh huh.

>   SAMMY
> What's it about?

>   RUDY
> My father.

Pause.

>   SAMMY
> What about your father?

>   RUDY
> It's just a made-up story about him.

>   SAMMY
> Can I read it when you're done?

>   RUDY
> It's not very good.

>   SAMMY
> Don't say that.

Rudy keeps writing.

INT. LIVING ROOM. LATER.

Sammy is smoking a cigarette and drinking a glass of wine and reading Rudy's story. It upsets her.

INT. SAMMY'S BEDROOM. LATER.

Sammy sits on the edge of her bed, not dialing the phone. She catches a glimpse of herself in her parents' floor-length mirror with the worn, heavy wooden frame. Against her better judgment she picks up the phone and dials.

INT. DAWSON'S GRILL. NIGHT.

Sammy and BOB STEEGERSON *are eating dinner at Dawson's, the only fancy restaurant in town. Bob is in his mid-thirties, a Realtor, a decent, ordinary guy.*

> SAMMY
>
> Anyway, Bob, it's sort of this adventure story, and Rudy's father is this secret agent or something, working for the government. . . . And it just made me feel weird. You know? Because I never really say much to him about Rudy Sr., because I don't know what to say. And I don't know whether I should just let him imagine whatever he wants to imagine, or whether I should sit him down sometime and tell him, you know, that his father is not such a nice person. You know?

> BOB
>
> Well . . . I don't know, Sammy. What have you told him already?

> SAMMY
>
> Not much. He knows I don't have the highest opinion of him. And he knows I don't want to see him or know anything about him, ever. But I tried to keep it kind of neutral. Anyway . . . I could go into a lot more detail, believe me.

BOB

Well . . . It's an interesting problem. But I don't really
know what to tell you. . . . It's a little outside my
personal field of expertise . . .

SAMMY

All right.

BOB

I'd be glad to give it some thought . . .

SAMMY

OK.

He is smiling at her.

SAMMY

What?

BOB

Nothing. . . . I'm just glad to see you. . . . I'm glad you
called me.

SAMMY

I bet you were surprised . . . !

BOB

Um—a little.

Bob drains his wineglass. Sammy cuts at her steak.

INT. BOB'S BEDROOM. NIGHT.

*Sammy and Bob lie in Bob's bed, a few minutes after having made
love. They are very far away from each other, but trying with difficulty not to let on.*

SAMMY

I should get going . . .

BOB

Really?

SAMMY

Yeah. . . . I've got the baby-sitter. . . . But . . . Thanks
for a lovely evening.

Oh. Thank *you*.

She kisses him. She tries to make it sexy, but he's not into it anymore and he politely restricts the kissing.

INT. SAMMY'S BATHROOM. NIGHT.

Sammy stands in her slip brushing her teeth in front of the mirror. She brushes vigorously, looking at herself while she brushes.

DISSOLVE TO:

EXT. STREET CORNER—WORCESTER, MASS. DAWN.

The corner window of a grim little apartment building on a very grim street in a grim little city.

INT. TERRY'S APARTMENT—WORCESTER, MASS. NIGHT.

A tiny apartment with a bed, chair, table, fridge, and not much else. One window has a broken pane and an old sheet neatly thumbtacked over it to keep the wind out.

TERRY PRESCOTT *comes in. He is twenty-five years old: a real mess with a certain natural appeal. He wears old jeans, very old hiking boots, and a lumberjack-style coat. He takes a wool hat off his head. His hair is longish and dirty.*

SHEILA SADLER *is sitting at the table by the fridge. She is barely eighteen, frail and damaged.*

> SHEILA
>
> Hey, Terry.

> TERRY
>
> Hey.

Terry looks at her and smiles encouragingly. She smiles back.

> SHEILA
>
> Where'd you get the hat?

> TERRY
>
> Oh, I got it on the street for a dollar.

SHEILA

It's nice.

TERRY

Well, you know, it's pretty much your standard woolen hat.

SHEILA

Yeah, I had a very similar reaction to it.

Sheila looks away. Silence.

TERRY

Can I get that money from you?

SHEILA

Yeah. Sorry.

As she opens her purse, Terry takes a few vague steps toward her. She takes out a tiny hippie-ish woven wallet and gives Terry all the money in it: a twenty and two ones.

TERRY

Is that all you have?

SHEILA

Yeah.

TERRY

Can you borrow some cash from your brother?

SHEILA

Um, yeah, but that would involve speaking to him.

TERRY

Well, I'm definitely gonna be gone for a couple of days at least, Sheila.

SHEILA

Why do you have to stay so long?

TERRY

Because my sister is
not a bank, you know?
I can't just show up
and ask her for—

SHEILA

You seem to think my
brother's a bank!

TERRY

Oh Sheila can we just cut out the puerile crap?! I'll be
back just as soon as I can. OK? I am not the kind of man
that everyone says I am.

SHEILA

I know you're not.

TERRY

I'll call you tonight.

Pause.

SHEILA

Don't you wanna tell me you love me?

TERRY

I love you.

SHEILA

That was really convincing.

TERRY

Well . . . I think after this is over you should seriously
consider moving back home.

SHEILA *(Short laugh)*

Oh, yeah.

TERRY *(Gives up)*

All right . . .

SHEILA

You gonna call tonight?

TERRY

Definitely.

She puts her arms around him and holds on.

EXT. NEW YORK STATE—MOUNTAINS—HIGHWAY. DAY.

Wide open shot of hilly country and a big sky overhead. A GREY-
HOUND BUS *drives into the shot along the curve of the highway.*

INT. BUS (MOVING)—BATHROOM. DAY.

Terry is seated on the toilet seat in the cramped bathroom smoking a joint. He takes a huge hit and holds it in for as long as humanly possible. He blows out what's left, takes another equally huge hit and holds it in.

EXT. LOCAL HIGHWAY. DAY.

The BUS WHOOSHES *along a smaller, heavily wooded roller-coaster road.*

INT. BUS (MOVING). DAY.

Terry looks out the window at the passing scenery. The sunlight flickers on his face.

POV TERRY: *The bus rolls past the hilltop cemetery.*

Terry shifts uncomfortably in his seat.

POV TERRY: THE "WELCOME TO SCOTTSVILLE" SIGN *whizzes by. Houses start dotting the side of the road.*

Terry starts getting very agitated.

EXT. MAIN STREET. DAY.

Terry stands at one end of Main Street, backpack over his shoulder, as the BUS DRIVES OFF. *He looks around at the town going about its Saturday afternoon business.*

INT. KITCHEN. SIMULTANEOUS.

Loud country-western music is blaring as Sammy, wearing an apron, sets a big vase of flowers on the kitchen table and hurries to the oven. There are also cookies, a pie, evidence of massive fancy cooking. She puts on her oven mitts and takes a lasagna out of the oven, as the phone rings. She picks up.

> SAMMY *(Into phone)*
> Hello? . . . TERRY! . . .

EXT. SAMMY'S HOUSE. DAY.

Sammy practically bursts out the front door. She has changed into nice clothes.

EXT. ALLEY. DAY.

Terry secrets himself in a small dark alley. He takes out his carefully wrapped half joint and lights it. SMOKING, *he looks at the sunlit slant of street beyond the alley.*

EXT. MAIN STREET. A FEW MOMENTS LATER.

Terry, fairly well stoned, walks along Main Street. A skinny man emerges from his hardware store to greet Terry and shake hands. Terry says "Hi," but keeps on walking. He passes some other people.

He almost runs right into SHERIFF DARRYL, *sixteen years fatter and grayer.*

> SHERIFF
>
> Whoa there!

> TERRY
>
> Sorry.

The Sheriff recognizes Terry and breaks into a big smile.

> SHERIFF
>
> God *damn!* Terry Prescott! How you doin'? Gimme a cuddle!

The Sheriff gives Terry a big bear hug. Terry is wasted and self-conscious but smiling. He pats the Sheriff's back.

> TERRY
>
> How you doin', Darryl?

> SHERIFF
>
> Which way you headed?

> TERRY
>
> I'm just goin' to see Sammy at Dawson's . . .

> SHERIFF
>
> Can I walk with you a little?

> TERRY
>
> Sure, yeah—

SHERIFF

So Sammy says you been out in *Alaska . . .* ?

TERRY

Yeah, I was workin' out there for a little while . . .

EXT. MAIN STREET. A FEW MOMENTS LATER.

The Sheriff walks along with Terry. Terry, very self-conscious about smelling like pot, fumbles to light a cigarette. The Sheriff does not seem to notice.

SHERIFF

—Sammy says she's gettin' postcards from all across the country.

TERRY

Yeah, I've been all over the place . . .

They stop outside Dawson's.

SHERIFF

Well, it's good to have you back here, I'll tell you that.

TERRY

Thanks, Darryl. Keep enforcing the peace.

SHERIFF

Well, that'll be a little harder now that you're home, but I'll do what I can.

TERRY

No, man, I'm reformed.

SHERIFF

Oh, yeah. Good to see you, kid.

TERRY

Thanks, Darryl.

Darryl walks away. Terry stands outside the restaurant looking for Sammy.

Behind him in the restaurant Sammy is sitting at a table, talking to the waitress.

She sees Terry and gets up immediately, smiling like crazy as she threads her way through the tables toward the door.

Terry turns and sees her. He breaks into a big smile, tosses his cigarette and goes into the restaurant. Through the window we see them make their way toward each other.

Sammy throws her arms around him. He hugs her back with a big involuntary smile as the GLASS DOOR *slowly* CLOSES.

INT. DAWSON'S—AT THEIR TABLE. A FEW MOMENTS LATER.

Terry is studying the menu, over-intently. Sammy is beaming at him.

                    TERRY
Sorry about yesterday—

                    SAMMY
I don't care—

                    TERRY
I was studying the bus description . . . and I just . . . I got on the wrong bus—I mean I missed my stop—

                    SAMMY
I don't care, Terry. I'm just so glad to see you . . . !

                    TERRY
I'm glad to see you too, Sammy. Um . . . are you coming from work?

                    SAMMY
Um, no, it's Saturday . . .

                    TERRY
Yeah, no, it's just . . . you're dressed so formally . . .

                    SAMMY
Oh. No. You know, I just thought I'd— You know I thought it was a special occasion . . . which it is . . .

                    TERRY
No, it's good. I thought I'd dress up too.

He gestures to his shitty clothes.

>SAMMY

That's OK. You look fine.

>TERRY *(A strange, unsuccessful joke)*

Yeah, this is the haute cuisine of garments.

>SAMMY

What?

>TERRY

Nothing, nothing . . . Um . . . So how are you?

>SAMMY

I'm fine.

>TERRY

How's Rudy?

>SAMMY

We're fine, Terry. How are *you*? *(Pause)* I mean—

>TERRY

Yeah . . .

>SAMMY

—Where have you *been* lately, Terry?

>TERRY

—I know, I haven't been—

>SAMMY

I got a postcard from you from Alaska . . . ?

>TERRY

Yeah, I was up there for a while . . .

>SAMMY

But that was in the *Fall,* Terry . . .

>TERRY

Yeah, I know I've been out of touch . . .

>SAMMY

I was a little worried. *(Pause)* I mean—

TERRY

Oh, I been a lotta different places. . . . Um . . . I went
down to Florida for a while. . . . I was doing some work
in Orlando. . . . I've been all over the place.

SAMMY

Well . . . I just wish you would have let me know you
were OK . . .

TERRY

Yeah. I didn't realize it'd been so long . . .

He looks around the restaurant.

SAMMY *(Beaming again)*
Are you gonna stay in town for a while?

TERRY

Well, I don't know. . . . I got all these things I gotta do
back in Worcester . . .

SAMMY

Oh . . .

TERRY

. . . Yeah, so I'm probably not gonna be able to stay
more than a day or so . . .

SAMMY

Oh . . . Well . . . That's all right . . . !

TERRY

. . . I'm kind of trying to keep to a schedule of sorts. It's
a long and worthy story but I won't trouble you with it
right now.

He twists around and looks all over the restaurant. She watches him.

SAMMY

Are you expecting someone?

TERRY

Who would I be expecting here?

SAMMY

You just keep looking around, that's all.

TERRY

No, I was just wondering if we could get some more refreshments, actually.

He laughs. Looks down. Silence. He looks up at her.

TERRY

I've actually got to confess to you, Sammy . . . that the reason you may not have heard from me for a little while is that I've been kind of unable to write . . . on account of the fact that I was in jail for a little while.

SAMMY

You were *what*?

A couple of people in the restaurant look at them. Terry notices but Sammy does not.

TERRY

Well, I did a little time, I guess, in Florida. For, uh, just for bullshit . . .

SAMMY

What?!

TERRY

It was just bullshit . . .

SAMMY

What did you do?

TERRY

I didn't do *any*thing. Does it occur to you that maybe I was *wronged*?

SAMMY

No!

TERRY

Well, could I please—

SAMMY

Oh my *God*!—

TERRY

Would you please let me—

SAMMY

—What *happened*?!

TERRY

I got into a fight in a bar down in Florida. Which I
was not the one who instigated it, at *all.* But they
worked up all this bullshit against me and they threw
me in the pen for three months. I didn't write you
because I didn't want you to get all upset about it.
I just figured you'd figure I was on the road for a little
while. I know it was stupid and I'm sorry. I really
didn't mean to make you worry. But you know what?
I can't run around all the time doin' stuff or not doin'
stuff because it's gonna make you *worry*! Because then
I come back here, and I tell you about my fuckin' . . .
traumas, and I get this wounded little "I've Let You
Down" bullshit, over and over again, and it really
just—*cramps* me! Like I just want to get out from *under*
it! . . . And here I am back in this fuckin' hole
explaining myself to you again!

SAMMY

OK— Can you please stop cursing at me?

TERRY

I mean, I realize I'm in no position to, uh, basically say
anything, *ever*— But it's not like I'm down there in
some redneck bar in Florida having an argument with
some stripper's boyfriend and I suddenly think, "Hey!
Maybe this'd be a good time to really stick it to Sammy
and get myself locked up for a few months."

SAMMY

I'm sorry.

TERRY

Me too, man. I mean "welcome home."

SAMMY

Hey— You don't write me for six *months,* I have no idea
where you are—

TERRY

I'm sorry—

SAMMY

—I don't know if you're alive or *dead*—

TERRY

I'm sorry—

SAMMY

—and then you show up out of nowhere and tell me you
were in *jail?*

TERRY

I'm sorry, I'm sorry, I'm sorry, Sammy, I'm really
sorry . . . !

The patrons are all either looking at them or trying not to look. Silence.

TERRY

Sammy . . .

SAMMY

What?

TERRY

Um . . . I'm in the midst of a slight predicament . . .

SAMMY

What do you need? Money?

TERRY

Um . . . Yeah . . . I'm broke. I gotta get back to
Worcester tomorrow. I got this girl there, and she's kind
of in a bad situation . . . ? I just need to borrow some
money. Whatever you can spare. *(Pause)* I'll pay you
back. . . . I'll pay you back, man.

SAMMY

I really wish Mom was here.

TERRY

So do I, man.

SAMMY

Nobody knows what to do with you.

TERRY

I know how they feel, man.

Silence, except for the sounds of the restaurant.

SAMMY

Terry? Can I ask you something?

TERRY

Sure.

SAMMY *(With some difficulty)*

Well—I mean, do you ever go to church anymore?

TERRY

Come on, Sammy, can we not talk about that shit?

SAMMY

Do you?

TERRY

Um— No, Sammy. I don't.

SAMMY

Can you tell me why not?

TERRY

Um, yeah. Because I think it's ridiculous.

SAMMY	TERRY
Well—can you tell me without like, denigrating what *I* believe in?	Because I think it's primitive, OK? I think it's a fairy tale.

SAMMY

Well—I mean, have you ever considered that maybe
that's part of what's making things so difficult for you?

TERRY

No.

SAMMY

—That you've lost hold of—well, not just your religious
feeling, but lost hold of any kind of anchor, any kind of
trust in anything. . . . I mean no wonder you drift
around so much. What could ever stop you? How would
you ever know if you had found the right thing?

TERRY

Well, uh, I'm not really looking for anything, man. I'm
just, like, trying to get on with it.

The WAITRESS *approaches with their salads.*

WAITRESS

Here we go . . .

She sets them down on the table.

SAMMY and TERRY

Thank you.

The WAITRESS *leaves. Silence. Terry picks at his salad. Sammy doesn't
touch hers. She watches him miserably.*

EXT. BANK—ATM. DAY.

*Terry watches while Sammy inserts her card in the ATM and punches
in her code. Terry waits. She punches in $300. The machine grinds out
her cash. She gives him the money.*

TERRY

Thank you, Sammy. . . . I'm really gonna pay this back.

She takes her card back and puts it back in her wallet.

INT. SAMMY'S CAR. DAY.

Sammy and Terry get in the car. Sammy isn't saying anything.

TERRY

Where we going?

To pick up Rudy.

She puts on her glasses and her seat belt. She won't look at him.

TERRY

Well . . . do you not even want me to visit now? 'Cause I can catch the bus at *five o'clock* if that's what you want.

SAMMY

Well, of course I want you to visit, you *idiot*! I've been looking forward to seeing you more than anything! I've been telling everyone I *know* that you were coming home! I cleaned the whole fucking house so it would look nice for you! I thought you were gonna stay for at least a few days! It didn't occur to me that you were just broke again. I wish you would have just sent me an *invoice*!

She stops. Terry is now totally contrite.

INT. BATHROOM. NIGHT.

Terry sits in the tub. Water drips from the faucet. He is staring blankly up at the pristine blue-and-white tiled wall and the neatly folded matching towels.

INT. LIVING ROOM. LATER.

Sammy and Rudy are in the living room. Rudy is playing with a Game Boy type game. In the b.g., TERRY *is dialing the* PHONE. *He looks clean and shaved, his hair is neatly combed.*

TERRY *(Into phone)*

Hi, is that Malcolm? . . . Hi, this is Terry Prescott? . . . I been trying to get ahold of Sheila and there's no answer, and I was just wondering if she— . . . She *what*? . . .

He sits down.

TERRY *(Into phone)*

When? . . . Well— Is she all right? . . . Well, could I talk to her? . . . Well, could you give her a message that I—

CLICK. *He is hung up on. He slowly* HANGS UP.

Sammy notices that something's wrong. He looks at her from across the room.

> TERRY
> That girl I'm with tried to kill herself.

> SAMMY
> What?

> TERRY
> She tried to kill herself.

INT. TERRY'S ROOM. NIGHT.

Terry is sitting on the bed, addressing an envelope to SHEILA. *He puts the $300 in the* ENVELOPE *and seals it. He sees Sammy standing in the doorway. He starts to unlace his boots.*

> SAMMY
> Do you have everything you need?

> TERRY
> I think so.

Sammy comes into the room and sits next to him. He is very busy with his laces.

> SAMMY
> What are you going to do?

> TERRY
> I don't know. Send the money I guess.

> SAMMY
> Maybe you should stay home for a little while, Terry.

> TERRY
> Yeah, maybe that'd be a good idea.

He starts crying. Sammy pats him.

EXT. SCOTTSVILLE CHURCH. DAY.

A bright, clear, blue-skied Sunday morning in Scottsville. Inside the little white church they're singing.

EXT. CHURCH. DAY.

People are filing out of the church. We also see a couple of the bank employees, including BRIAN *and his very pretty six months'* PREGNANT *wife,* NANCY. *We find* SAMMY *and* RUDY. *Sammy is chatting to some neighbors. Rudy is bored out of his mind, waiting for her.*

INT. SAMMY'S HOUSE—LIVING ROOM. DAY.

Terry is lying on the sofa, smoking, with his feet up and boots on, watching Sunday morning TV. *On the coffee table are his dirty ashtray, dirty bowl and spoon, Rice Krispies box and a milk carton.*

EXT. SAMMY'S HOUSE. NIGHT.

Crickets buzz loudly outside the house.

INT. STAIRS. NIGHT.

Sammy, in her bathrobe, comes down the stairs into the living room. Terry is on the sofa playing with Rudy's Game Boy. He barely looks up when she speaks to him.

SAMMY

I'm going to bed. Do you have everything you need?

TERRY

Yeah. Thanks.

SAMMY

Good night.

TERRY

Good night.

Pause.

SAMMY

Terry, I'm really glad you're home.

Terry tries to smile at her.

TERRY

Yeah, me too, Sammy.

He goes back to his game. She hesitates, then heads back up the stairs.

INT. SAMMY'S KITCHEN. DAY.

Sammy, Terry and Rudy sit at the kitchen table. Sammy is dressed for work. Rudy is dressed for school. Terry is also fully dressed, drinking the last dregs of a mug of coffee. He is tired, but listening to Sammy very carefully, as if receiving difficult and critical instructions.

SAMMY

OK. So we'll drop Rudy off at the bus, then all you have to do is drop me off at the bank, and just pick Rudy up at 3:30 in front of town hall, and drive him over to Carol's house. And that's it. She's on Harvey Lane, right past where the Dewitts used to live.

TERRY

OK.

SAMMY

Rudy knows where she lives.

Terry glances at Rudy, then back at Sammy.

TERRY
OK.

INT. BANK—MABEL'S DESK. DAY.

Sammy walks past MABEL'S DESK, *carrying a big stack of files. She drops three of them on the desk.* MABEL *is typing away at her* PC. *The colors are a garish* PURPLE *background with* GREEN *letters.*

SAMMY

God, Mabel, don't those colors hurt your eyes?

MABEL

Oh no, they keep me fresh.

Sammy proceeds down the hall and into—

INT. BRIAN'S OFFICE. DAY.

Brian is at his desk, busy working between stacks of papers. She knocks on the open door.

BRIAN

Yeah! *(Looks up)* Hi, Sammy. What can I do for you?

SAMMY

Um, Brian? Did you want us to turn this time sheet in at the end of the day, or do you want it at the end of the week . . . ?

BRIAN

Oh, yeah, end of the day'll be fine.

SAMMY

Seems like an awful lot of extra paperwork . . .

Brian hesitates, shrugs and smiles.

BRIAN

I like paperwork.

Sammy looks at him with a blank smile.

INT. BANK—SAMMY'S DESK. A MOMENT LATER.

Sammy sits down at her desk and notices the time: 3:30. She reaches for the phone, then decides not to call.

EXT. SCOTTSVILLE—MAIN STREET. DAY.

The CLOCK *on the front of the* TOWN HALL *reads 3:31.*

The SCHOOL BUS *pulls up across from the town hall and disgorges a handful of kids. Rudy comes out with his knapsack, looking around . . .*

POV RUDY: *Terry, across the street, sits on the hood of Sammy's car, smoking.*

Rudy walks over to him.

> RUDY
>
> You showed up.

> TERRY
>
> Looks that way.

INT. SAMMY'S CAR (MOVING). DAY.

Terry and Rudy drive in silence. Terry glances at Rudy.

> TERRY
>
> Put on your seat belt.

> RUDY
>
> It pushes on my neck.

> TERRY
>
> What?

> RUDY
>
> It pushes on my neck. It's uncomfortable.

> TERRY
>
> Well, when somebody slams into us and you go sailin'
> through the windshield, that's liable to be
> uncomfortable too. So put on your seat belt.

Rudy puts on his seat belt.

> RUDY
>
> Mom's parents died in a car accident.

> TERRY
>
> I know. They're my parents too.

                    RUDY

They are?

                    TERRY

Well, yeah. Your mom is my sister.

                    RUDY

Yeah, I know.

                    TERRY

So that means we have the same parents.

                    RUDY

Oh yeah.

They drive in silence for a moment. Terry glances down at Rudy.

INT. BANK—SAMMY'S DESK. DAY.

Sammy, laden with files, plops down at her desk as Mabel is passing by. Mabel puts a phone message down in front of her.

                    MABEL

Um—Carol just called. She said Terry and Rudy never showed up at her house?

                    SAMMY

You've got to be kidding me.

A MOMENT LATER: *Brian, talking to an employee, sees Sammy, across the bank, hurrying out the employees' exit.*

                    BRIAN

Hey, Sammy?

Sammy doesn't hear and exits.

EXT. ORRIN'S BACKYARD. DAY.

Terry and Rudy are banging nails with RAY, *a young guy Terry's age. Terry, hammering with swift, accurate blows, glances up and watches Rudy for a second. Rudy is hammering away with no great skill.*

                    TERRY

Hey. Look.

He moves Rudy's hand down toward the end of the handle.

> TERRY

You hold it further down, you're gonna get a lot more power. You should be able to put that nail down with two or three hits. Look:

With two swift strokes he drives the nail flush into the wood.

> TERRY

Try it.

> RUDY

That's not the way I hold it.

> TERRY

Well, the way you hold it is wrong.

> RUDY

Why can't I just do it my own way?

Terry looks at him unsympathetically for a moment.

> TERRY *(Shrugs)*

You can.

He goes back to work. Rudy resumes hammering. After a moment he switches his grip and starts hammering Terry's way. Terry looks up and watches him.

EXT. IN FRONT OF ORRIN'S HOUSE. A MOMENT LATER.

Sammy pulls up, fast, and gets out of the car. Hearing the hammering from the backyard, she walks quickly around the side of the house and stops short when she sees Rudy hammering happily away with Terry and Ray.

She watches them working, unobserved, with mixed annoyance and relief, and finally with quiet pleasure, because it's a very cheerful sight.

INT. BANK. DAY.

Half the staff has gone home. Sammy, in her coat, picks a NOTE up off her CHAIR. It reads:

"SAMMY, PLEASE SEE ME A.S.A.P!!!—BRIAN"

INT. BRIAN'S OFFICE. A MOMENT LATER.

Sammy stands in front of Brian's desk.

> SAMMY
>
> Brian? Did you want to see me?

> BRIAN
>
> Yeah. I was kind of wondering what happened to you today.

> SAMMY
>
> Oh— Didn't Mabel— I had a false alarm about my son . . .

> BRIAN
>
> Yeah, I kind of thought you were gonna work that out.

SAMMY	BRIAN
Well, I did work it out—more or less—	Then why're you running outta here in the middle of the day without a word of explanation to me, Sammy?

> SAMMY
>
> Brian, don't yell at me.

> BRIAN
>
> I'm—I'm not yelling. I'm just gettin' a little frustrated here.

> SAMMY
>
> Well Brian:

> BRIAN
>
> Sorry, could you close the door please?

Sammy closes the door.

INT. DINING ROOM. NIGHT.

Sammy, Terry and Rudy sit at dinner. The atmosphere is lively and cheerful.

SAMMY

. . . And Eddy Dwyer lives in Buffalo, with his wife and two sons, if you can believe it.

TERRY

That is depressing.

SAMMY

Why?

TERRY

He just never struck me as the marrying type, that's all.

RUDY

Who are you talking about?

TERRY

Wild kids we used to know.

RUDY

Were you a wild kid?

TERRY

Not compared to your Mom.

RUDY

Yeah, right.

TERRY

You don't believe me?

RUDY

No.

TERRY

Ask her.

RUDY

Mom, were you?

SAMMY

No comment.

Rudy is amazed. Terry looks at him like, "Told you so."

INT. SAMMY'S BEDROOM. NIGHT.

Sammy is asleep in bed.

INT. RUDY'S BEDROOM. NIGHT.

Rudy is asleep in bed.

INT. BAR. NIGHT.

Terry sits at the bar, drinking beer. There are a few locals in the place, but it's pretty dead. He looks around; his energy is too restless for the near-empty bar.

INT. RUDY'S BEDROOM. NIGHT.

The DOOR OPENS, *and* TERRY COMES IN, *smoking a cigarette. He's plastered. He looks around the room. Looks at Rudy's toys. Picks up some superhero comics and sits on Rudy's bed. Then he spies Rudy's* COMPOSITION BOOK, *picks it up and starts reading it.*

> RUDY *(O.C.)*
> What are you doing?

Terry looks up. Rudy is half-sitting up in bed.

> TERRY
> Oh—Just readin' some of your compositions.

> RUDY
> Why are you *smoking*?

> TERRY
> Um . . . Because it's bad. Don't ever do it.

> RUDY
> I won't.

> TERRY
> You know this used to be my room?

> RUDY
> Yeah . . . *(Pause)* Do you want it back?

> TERRY
> No.

Rudy is very relieved. Terry keeps reading. Rudy watches him.

RUDY

Did you fight in Vietnam?

TERRY

No. I wasn't even born yet.

RUDY

Were you ever in the army?

TERRY

No.

RUDY

My father was in the army.

TERRY

I know. Unfortunately he didn't fight in Vietnam either.

RUDY

Were you friends with him?

TERRY

Not really. We had some friends in common, I guess.
. . . I didn't like him very much.

RUDY

Why not?

TERRY

Well, he wasn't very likable.

RUDY

Why do you say that?

TERRY

I don't know. He was always— He always had to be
better than you at everything. You know. Like if you
were all playing basketball or something, everybody's
havin' like a friendly game and he's like ready to kill
somebody if his team didn't win. Or like if you told like
a joke or a story, he always had to tell a better one?
Kinda gets annoying after a while. Plus it was pretty

scummy how he split on your mom and you. . . . He was a prick. Probably still a prick. Fortunately for you though, your mom is like, the greatest. So you had some bad luck and you had some good luck. *(Pause)* You mind if I ask you a personal question?

RUDY

I don't know.

TERRY

Do you like it here? I mean, in Scottsville?

RUDY

Yeah . . . ?

TERRY

Why?

RUDY

I don't know. My friends are here. . . . I like the scenery. . . . I don't know.

TERRY

I know, I know, but it's so . . . There's nothing to *do* here.

RUDY

Yes there is.

TERRY

No there isn't, man! It's *narrow.* It's *dull.* It's a dull, narrow town full of dull, narrow people who don't know anything except . . . what things are like right around here. They have no perspective whatsoever. No scope. They might as well be living in the nineteenth century because they have no idea what's going on, and if you try to tell 'em that, they wanna fuckin' kill you.

RUDY

What are you talking about?

TERRY

I don't know . . .

Terry lies on his back and smokes.

> TERRY
>
> You're a good kid.

INT. BANK—SAMMY'S DESK. MORNING.

There's a NOTE *on Sammy's chair.*

"SAMMY, PLEASE SEE ME—BRIAN"

Sammy, just arrived at work and still in her coat, looks down at the note.

INT. BANK—BRIAN'S OFFICE. DAY.

Sammy listens to Brian.

> BRIAN
>
> Yeah. This doesn't apply to you directly, Sammy, but I've noticed that some of the employees have their PC monitors set with all kinds of crazy colors. . . . Purple and polka dots or what have you. And it's not a big deal, but really, this is a bank. You know? It's not really appropriate. So I'm just asking that people stick to a more quote unquote normal range of colors in future . . .

Sammy looks at him blankly.

> BRIAN
>
> Like I say, it doesn't really apply to you.

> SAMMY
>
> No, my computer palette's pretty conservative.

INT. BANK—MABEL'S DESK. DAY.

Mabel is typing angrily at a GRAY SCREEN *with* BLACK LETTERS. *Sammy walks by. Mabel is so mad she doesn't even look up.*

INT. BANK—SAMMY'S DESK. DAY.

Sammy sits agitated for a moment. She makes a decision, picks up the phone and dials.

INT. BOB'S OFFICE. SIMULTANEOUS.

Bob is in his little realty office with two CLIENTS, *a husband and wife. He picks up his* RINGING PHONE.

> BOB *(Into phone)*
>
> Bob Steegerson.

> SAMMY *(On phone)*
>
> What are you wearing?

> BOB *(Into phone)*
>
> Mom?

Sammy LAUGHS.

INT. SAMMY'S HOUSE—DOWNSTAIRS HALL. NIGHT.

Terry is holding a broom looking up at the ceiling. Sammy passes by and stops.

> SAMMY
>
> What's up?

Terry taps the broom handle against the ceiling.

> TERRY
>
> Do you know you have an enormous leak from the upstairs hall?

He pokes again. A portion of the ceiling collapses on his head in wet chunks of plaster and muck.

> SAMMY
>
> Um, yeah, thanks, I did.

INT. SAMMY'S ROOM. NIGHT.

Sammy, in front of the mirror, finishes dolling herself up for her date. O.C. *we hear loud banging. Sammy puts on her earrings and goes into—*

INT. HALL. CONTINUOUS.

> SAMMY
>
> Are you guys sure you're gonna be OK?

TERRY

Yes. Yes.

Sammy approaches RUDY *and* TERRY. *They are bent over a big nasty trench in the floorboard. There are wood shavings and greasy pipe segments all over, and black smeary smudges on the walls nearby.*

SAMMY

What is happening here?

TERRY

It's just— The problem is that the pipe is corroded all the way along the length of the hall. So every time I put in a new piece it starts leaking further down.

SAMMY

Why don't I just call the plumber?

TERRY

Why? He's not gonna do anything different than what I'm doing.

RUDY *(Happily)*

Yeah. We're making it *worse*!

TERRY

No we're not. Shut up.

Terry yanks the wrench and a SPRAY *of* FILTHY WATER *comes out of the pipe and splatters the wallpaper and pictures and Sammy with gritty gray water. She looks at them.*

SAMMY

Thank you. Thank you both.

INT. HALLWAY. NIGHT.

Bob and Sammy—cleaned up and wearing a different outfit—are bustling out the front door. Terry stands by.

SAMMY

Now, call if there's any problem, and if I'm not there, I'm either on my way or on my way back home.

TERRY

OK.

Sammy gets into her coat. Bob opens the front door.

SAMMY *(To TERRY)*
So lights out at ten . . . and
don't spend the whole night
watching TV.

TERRY
Nice to meet you, Bob.

BOB
You too.

TERRY *(To SAMMY)*
What's your idea of the whole night?

SAMMY

Two hours tops.

Bob holds the door for Sammy and smiles at her. There is some confusion about who should go out first. Finally she goes and Bob follows. The atmosphere between them is fairly awkward.

INT. SAMMY'S HOUSE. NIGHT.

Terry and Rudy are watching TV from the sofa.

TERRY
What's your feeling about Bob?

RUDY
I don't really know him that well.

Terry looks at his watch.

TERRY
I have bad news for you.

He picks up the remote . . .

RUDY
No . . . !

. . . and turns off the TV. They sit there in the sudden silence.

RUDY
Great. What are we supposed to do now?

TERRY

Do you know how to play pool?

RUDY

I've played it.

EXT. THE WILD MOOSE. NIGHT.

The Wild Moose is a noisy roadside bar sitting under the stars. Terry and Rudy get out of the car. Rudy looks apprehensive.

RUDY

I don't think they let kids in there.

TERRY

Well, we're not allowed to watch any more TV, so it's this or nothing. . . . But if we run into any trouble, let me do the talking.

RUDY

OK.

Terry swings the door open.

INT. THE WILD MOOSE. NIGHT.

POV RUDY: *A lot of men and women at the bar or in booths, eating and drinking. Smoky, crowded and very loud. As he follows Terry through the crowd various patrons notice him—some of the looks are friendly, some blank, some cold, i.e., what's a kid doing in here?*

AT THE POOL TABLE: *Terry and Rudy stand side by side facing the players and waiting players gathered around the table. Terry waves a few bills.*

TERRY

I got a hundred bucks here says me and my nephew can beat anybody in here. Only we gotta get the next game 'cause he's gotta be in bed by ten o'clock.

A MOMENT LATER: RUDY, *very nervous, and the 1st Pool Player are side by side shooting for break. Terry is behind Rudy coaching him.*

TERRY

Just hit it nice and soft . . . Nice and soft.

They hit the balls. Rudy just clips his ball and it doesn't go anywhere. 1st Pool Player's ball hits the opposite bank and comes almost all the way back.

> RUDY *(To TERRY)*
>
> Sorry.

> TERRY
>
> God damn, Rudy. I thought you said you could play.

Rudy doesn't answer. Terry winks at him.

A MOMENT LATER: 1ST POOL PLAYER BREAKS—*WHACK!*—*The balls scatter. Nothing drops.* TERRY *steps up to the table, chalking up his cue.*

> TERRY
>
> Boys, it's all over but the cryin'.

QUICK CUTS: *Of Terry running the table and everyone watching. Three-ball in the side. One-ball in the corner. Nine-ball off three cushions and into the corner, and the eleven-ball into the side. Rudy watches him.*

INT. BOB'S APARTMENT. NIGHT.

Bob and Sammy sit at Bob's dining room table. The little bachelor apartment looks pretty good. Tablecloth, candles, wine, everything. Bob has just dropped a huge bombshell.

> SAMMY
>
> Bob . . . Are you serious?

> BOB
>
> Yeah.

> SAMMY
>
> I . . . I don't know what to say. I—

> BOB
>
> I mean, I know I haven't exactly been the most . . . decisive . . . guy. In the past . . . I don't know: I'm tired of foolin' around. And I love you.

> SAMMY
>
> I . . . I'm totally . . . I don't know what to say.

BOB

Well, you could always say "Yes." *(Pause)* Or you could think about it first.

SAMMY

That's it: I want to think about it.

BOB

OK . . . Fair enough.

INT. WILD MOOSE. NIGHT.

Terry has sunk everything but the eight ball. He leans over to sink it. It's a fairly easy shot. He lines it up carefully, and deliberately shoots it so it stops two inches from the corner pocket.

TERRY

Ohhhh!

A FEW MOMENTS LATER: *Terry and Rudy sit side by side watching as the 2nd Pool Player passes back and forth between them and the camera, running the table. "Oohs" and "All rights" emit from the spectators.*

Sudden silence. Then the clack of the balls connecting. A great common GROAN *goes up.* RUDY *looks up at Terry.*

TERRY

It's all yours, baby.

Rudy looks at the TABLE: *The eight-ball is two inches off the corner. The cue ball is a few inches away from it. A piece of cake, for an adult. Rudy looks deeply unconfident.*

He gets up and tries to line up the eight-ball. Terry is right next to him.

TERRY

Just make sure to hit it really gentle. But firm. And hit it a little low so you get some backspin. Don't even hit it. Just *kiss* it.

A long moment.

RUDY

What do you mean, kiss it?

TERRY

I mean *tap* it. Firm but very, very softly. And don't shoot until you *know* it's going in. OK?

RUDY

OK.

Everyone is relatively quiet. Rudy takes a few practice strokes and then hits the cue ball, straight, but too softly. It crawls toward the eight and taps it toward the corner, slower and slower, hangs there, and DROPS.

A GENERAL "HEYYY!" GOES UP *and everyone claps and cheers. Terry grabs Rudy. Rudy smiles, ecstatic.*

TERRY

That was great!

AT THE BAR: *Darryl the* SHERIFF, *in his civvies, drinking a pint of beer, notices Rudy and Terry.*

AT THE POOL TABLE: *Terry picks Rudy up and turns him upside down. Rudy laughs.*

EXT. SAMMY'S HOUSE. NIGHT.

The house is dark. Terry and Rudy are walking from the car to the house.

RUDY

We *creamed* those guys! We *creamed* them!

TERRY *(Stopping suddenly)*

Shh . . . ! Don't move.

They listen. A CAR *is* COMING.

TERRY

It's them!

They break for the door, Terry fumbling for his key. He gets the door open.

> TERRY
>
> Go! Go! Go!

He and Rudy run inside the house. The lights go on. BOB'S CAR *pulls into the* DRIVEWAY.

INT. THE HOUSE—FRONT DOOR. SIMULTANEOUS.

Rudy runs up the stairs.

> TERRY
>
> Wait a minute, gimme your jacket!

Rudy tries to take his jacket off fast but gets his arm caught in the sleeve. He tries to shake it off.

> TERRY
>
> What are you doing?

> RUDY
>
> I can't get my sleeve out . . . !

They HEAR *Bob's* CAR DOORS SLAM. *Terry makes a comic panicked face and leaps up the stairs two at a time.*

OUTSIDE THE HOUSE: *Sammy waves to Bob. Bob waves back as he drives off. Sammy goes to the front door, opens it:*

Terry and Rudy are in a giggly tangled panicked heap at the top of the stairs, shaking Rudy's arm and sleeve, frantically trying to get the jacket off.

Sammy comes in. They freeze.

> SAMMY
>
> What is going on in here?

> TERRY
>
> Um—We were just out doing some star-gazing, and, uh, Rudy lost track of the time. Which I totally warned him about. *(To Rudy)* You are a bad kid.

INT. BATHROOM. LATER.

Rudy is brushing his teeth. Terry pokes his head in.

> TERRY *(In a low voice)*
> Hey: I think it's OK. Just don't tell her where we went,
> 'cause she'll be really mad at me. OK?

> RUDY
> I won't.

> TERRY *(Suddenly dark)*
> Hey—I'm not kidding, Rudy.

> RUDY
> I won't!

Terry gives him a "You better not" look, then leaves. Rudy continues brushing his teeth.

INT. RUDY'S ROOM. NIGHT.

Sammy is tucking Rudy in, stroking his hair.

> SAMMY
> Did you know *my* Mommy used to take me and Uncle
> Terry out at night to look at the constellations?

> RUDY
> Yeah.

> SAMMY
> Did you see that one, what's the one— It looks like a
> big "W"? Cassiopeia?

> RUDY
> Yeah.

INT. HALL. NIGHT.

Sammy comes out of Rudy's room, smiling. It's dark. She sees a LIGHT on under TERRY'S DOOR. She walks toward it and steps into the TRENCH, falling down violently.

SAMMY

Ow! Shit!

INT. BATHROOM. NIGHT.

Terry is putting a butterfly Band-Aid on Sammy's wound. It's a nasty, bloody gash, just shy of needing stitches.

SAMMY

I've got a great idea. Why don't you let me call the plumber?

TERRY

Do whatever you want.

SAMMY

Oh, does that make you *mad*?

TERRY

No . . .

INT. SAMMY'S ROOM. NIGHT.

RAIN *patters on the* ROOF *as Sammy* LIMPS *back and forth across the room changing into her nightgown.*

EXT. TERRY'S WINDOW. NIGHT.

Terry is smoking pot with his head and shoulders stuck outside the window. RAIN FALLS *on his* HEAD.

DISSOLVE TO:

EXT. BANK. MORNING.

Early morning. The RAIN *is still falling. Only a few cars are in the employee parking lot yet.*

INT. BANK—BRIAN'S OFFICE. DAY.

The RAIN *runs down Brian's office window.* BRIAN, *in a wet raincoat, turns on his light.*

A MOMENT LATER: *Brian turns on his* PC. *The* SCREEN *lights up. The* COLORS *are a garish* GREEN *and* ORANGE.

CUT TO:

LATER: SAMMY *and* BRIAN *are both on their feet. The door is closed.*

> SAMMY
>
> Brian, get off my ass!

> BRIAN
>
> Excuse me?

> SAMMY
>
> I didn't change the colors on your stupid computer screen.

> BRIAN
>
> Well, that's all you gotta say!

> SAMMY *(On "that's")*
> There is nothing wrong with
> the work I do here. I have
> been doing just fine, the
> whole time before you came
> here— And if you think
> that riding people in
> this petty, ridiculous
> way is the way to improve
> service in this bank or
> anywhere else I think
> you're out of your mind!

> BRIAN
> I didn't say there was.
>
> Could I please—
>
> Could I please—

Pause.

> BRIAN
>
> May I respond?

> SAMMY
>
> No, that's really all I have to—

> BRIAN
>
> May I respond? *(Beat)* First of all, I don't appreciate
> being spoken to with that kind of language. That's not
> the way I talk to you, and I'd appreciate it if you
> wouldn't talk that way to me—

SAMMY

Well—

BRIAN

Second of all, if you say you didn't change the colors on my computer screen, then of course I accept your answer. But you and I are gonna have to find a way to work together—

SAMMY

Brian—

BRIAN

But that's not gonna happen with the attitude, it's not gonna happen with the lateness, it's not gonna happen by fighting me every step of the way— OK, well not you, you're not late, but too much of that stuff goes on around here—

SAMMY

I am not late and I do not have an attitude—

Well then don't tell me I'm late if I'm not late!

BRIAN

I'd really like to finish!

OUTSIDE BRIAN'S OFFICE: *The whole staff is listening to the muffled raised* VOICES *from inside the office.*

MABEL *especially is listening guiltily.*

EXT. MAIN STREET. DAY.

The rain falls on Main Street.

EXT. ORRIN'S BACKYARD. DAY.

The rain comes down hard on Orrin's construction project. Tarps cover everything. No work today.

EXT. MAIN STREET—LUNCH PLACE. DAY.

The rain comes down on the SHERIFF, *looking through the restaurant* WINDOW *at* SAMMY, *eating lunch alone at the counter. He goes inside,*

shakes the rain off himself and goes over to her. They start talking. We
HEAR:

> SAMMY

They were *where?*

INT. SAMMY'S HOUSE—LIVING ROOM. DAY.

The RAIN *on the roof makes a sleepy, pleasant country sound.*

TERRY *is lying on the sofa, smoking a joint, watching* TV, *in a funk.*
O.C. *we* LOUD BANGING ON THE PIPES.

LATER: A YOUNG PLUMBER, *about Terry's age, comes thumping down
the stairs and goes into the living room, carrying his toolbox. Terry
looks up at him.*

> PLUMBER

OK, you're all set.

Terry glares at him. The plumber turns and goes out.

EXT. BUS STOP. DAY.

RUDY *is* WAITING *in a doorway for Terry. He is wet and cold. The*
RAIN *pours down.*

INT. BANK. DAY.

Brian is showing his wife, NANCY, *the bank. He is very solicitous of
her, nervously introducing her to the employees, who are not responding
very warmly. Nancy is not in a warm mood either; she's very testy with
Brian.*

> BRIAN

This is Chuck. Chuck, this is my wife, Nancy.

> CHUCK

Hello.

> NANCY

Nice to meet you.

> BRIAN

This is Mabel . . .

Hi.

NANCY

Nice to meet you.

SAMMY, *at her desk, watches Brian and Nancy make their progress through the bank. Nobody is being very friendly, and Brian suddenly seems awkward and vulnerable. Brian and Nancy reach Sammy's desk.*

BRIAN

This is Sammy, our lending officer. Sammy, this is my wife, Nancy.

SAMMY *(Friendly)*

Hi. It's nice to meet you.

NANCY

Brian— I gotta sit down.

BRIAN

Sure— Let's go in my office.

He glances nervously at Sammy as he leads Nancy away from her desk and toward his office. He murmurs something to Nancy, who responds in a low but very testy voice:

NANCY

I'm *fine . . .* !

She roughly pulls her arm away from his. Sammy watches them go into his office.

EXT. MAIN STREET. DAY.

Rudy trudges resolutely through the pouring rain toward the center of town. He is completely drenched.

INT. BRIAN'S OFFICE. DAY.

Sammy knocks on Brian's open door.

SAMMY

Brian . . . ?

Yeah.

RUDY *(O.C.)*

Mom!

Sammy sees to her left, down the hallway—

SAMMY

Rudy!

Rudy is at the end of the hall, drenched and shivering, but cheerful.

EXT. EMPLOYEE PARKING LOT. DAY.

Rudy is in the car, somewhat dried off, waiting. Sammy and Terry stand in the employee entrance doorway.

SAMMY

Look, I'm glad you guys are getting along so well—like, you have no *idea*—but if I can't rely on you to remember to get him once a *day* . . .

TERRY

You can!

SAMMY

—And what are you doing taking him to play *pool* in the middle of the night, and then telling him to *lie* to me about it?

Pause.

TERRY

I don't know.

INT./EXT. SAMMY'S CAR/CAROL'S DRIVEWAY. DAY.

Terry and Rudy pull up in front of the driveway. Terry is in a silent rage. The rain has let up.

TERRY

Get out of the car.

RUDY

What are we doing?

TERRY

You're going to Carol's house and I'm going home.

RUDY

Why can't I come with you?

TERRY

Because if you're such a baby you gotta tell your *Mommy* about us playin' pool when I totally asked you not to, and I gotta listen to her shit all day, then you're goin' to the baby-sitter's so you can stay at the baby house.

RUDY

But I didn't tell her!

TERRY

You know what? Don't even fuckin' talk to me.

RUDY

I didn't!

TERRY

Just get out of the car.

He leans over Rudy roughly and pushes open the door. Rudy gets out of the car and marches down the long driveway. He bursts into tears.

Terry watches him go, then drives off.

INT. BANK—HALL. A FEW MOMENTS LATER.

Sammy walks through the empty bank hall and into Brian's office. Brian is at his desk.

> BRIAN
> You're working late.

> SAMMY
> How did your wife like the bank?

> BRIAN
> Oh, fine. She wasn't feeling so great.

> SAMMY
> That's too bad.

> BRIAN
> No—I don't mean— She's not ill. She's just . . . I don't know . . .

> SAMMY
> Pregnant?

> BRIAN
> That's it. She's pregnant.

> SAMMY
> It can make you kind of cranky.

> BRIAN
> Yeah . . .

Pause.

> BRIAN
> Listen, I'm sorry we've been stepping on each other's toes— I—I'm not actually that bad a guy—

> SAMMY
> Yeah, I am too . . .

SAMMY

I know you're not, Brian, but you're driving everybody crazy.

BRIAN

Well, I—I'm just trying to do my best here— And I'm gettin' it from all sides.

SAMMY

I know you are . . .

BRIAN

Anyway . . . We'll work it out . . .

SAMMY

Well . . . I could use a beer.

BRIAN

I could use a tranquilizer.

INT. PUB. NIGHT.

Brian and Sammy sit at a table in the corner of the dimly lit pub. It's a medium noisy place with various locals drinking beers and eating hamburgers and chicken dinners.

SAMMY

Last I heard, Rudy's Dad was living over in Auburn. But that was last year.

BRIAN

Must be so tough raising a kid on your own . . . Although I'm beginning to get the idea my wife wouldn't mind a crack at it.

SAMMY

Oh . . . It's just the hormones.

BRIAN

Well, no, it isn't. But never mind.

The waitress brings them two boilermakers.

SAMMY and BRIAN

Thanks.

She leaves. Sammy and Brian pick up their shots.

BRIAN

Well, here's to improved employee-management
relations.

SAMMY

Amen.

They click shot glasses and drink.

SAMMY

You can't judge all of Scottsville by the people in that
bank, believe me.

BRIAN

Well— Let's—Let's not talk about the bank.

SAMMY

OK.

BRIAN

Let's just forget about the bank for tonight.

SAMMY

Good idea.

They sip their drinks, smiling. Sammy looks at him appraisingly.

INT./EXT. BRIAN'S CAR/WOODED ROAD. NIGHT.

*Sammy and Brian are making out in the front seat of his car. This goes
on for a while, getting heavier and heavier.*

BRIAN

Sammy?

SAMMY

Yeah?

BRIAN

I want you to tell me who changed the colors on my
computer screen.

SAMMY

I'll *never* tell.

They start kissing again in the cramped space. Brian bangs his head. They laugh.

EXT. OUTSIDE THE CAR. CONTINUOUS.

We pull back and away from the car. The sodden trees spout faucets of water down on the car.

INT. KITCHEN. NIGHT.

The kitchen is dark. Sammy comes in, her hair a little wet, and turns on the light. She goes to the telephone.

There's a NOTE *in Terry's handwriting:*

"BOB CALLED."

TERRY *(O.C.)*

Where were *you?*

Sammy jumps, startled. Terry is in the kitchen doorway.

SAMMY

Nowhere. I had dinner with my boss.

TERRY

Kind of a late dinner, ain't it?

SAMMY

Yeah. How was Rudy?

TERRY

Fine.

SAMMY

Did the plumber come?

TERRY

Yes, the fucking plumber came.

SAMMY

Terry— Give me a *break*!!!

Pause.

TERRY

What's the matter with *you*?

SAMMY

Nothing. I'm just tired.

TERRY

You want to smoke some pot?

SAMMY

No I don't. Why, you got some?

EXT. PORCH. NIGHT.

Sammy and Terry stand side by side on the porch, passing a joint back and forth. It has stopped raining but the trees and roof are still dripping. The crickets are chirping loudly.

SAMMY

So . . . Bob asked me to marry him.

TERRY

Wow. *(Pause)* Are you going to?

SAMMY

I don't know. If he'd've asked me this time last year I would have probably said yes. But the minute he said it, I don't know, I felt like somebody was trying to strangle me.

TERRY

Well . . . bad sign.

SAMMY

I know. *(Pause)* Plus, Terry . . . *(Whispers)* I fucked my boss . . . !

TERRY

What?

SAMMY

I know! And his wife is six months pregnant.

TERRY

Jesus *Christ,* Sammy . . . !

SAMMY

I know, I know.

He passes her the joint. She declines. He puffs away. The water drips off the porch and the crickets chirp. She puts her head on his shoulder. He puts one arm around her and puffs away with the joint in his free hand.

SAMMY

Terry, I'm sorry I got so mad before. I just don't want him, you know—terrified of *"telling,"* if there's—

TERRY

Uh, well, that's not really his problem, Sammy.

Sammy straightens up.

SAMMY

Oh really? What's his problem?

TERRY

His problem is that he's like totally sheltered because you treat him like he's three, instead of eight, so that's how he behaves.

SAMMY

Oh yeah? And how do you think he should behave?

TERRY

I think he shouldn't have to run and tell his *Mommy* every time he does something she might not like, for one thing.

SAMMY

Uh huh. And what do you—

TERRY *(On "and")*

I mean I took him to play pool! It was a little clandestine thing we did for fun! It wasn't like a big *secret,* I mean who cares? I was actually trying to be *nice* to him. But he's so freaked out that he disobeyed your *orders* that he has to fuckin' squeal on me and I have to listen to your fuckin' shit all day when I didn't even fuckin' do anything!

First of all, he didn't tell me anything: *Darryl* did. OK?
Second of all, I don't really give a shit if you took him to
play pool: I was mad at you because you left him
standing at the bus stop in the *rain.* But no, I *don't* want
you telling him not to *squeal,* because I don't want him
put in that position!

TERRY *(Losing ground)*

Well . . . that . . . is a perfect example of what I'm
talking about.

SAMMY

You are an idiot.

They stand apart now. Silence.

TERRY

Darryl told you?

SAMMY

Yes!

They stand there. The rain gutters drip.

INT. BANK. MORNING.

*Sammy, coat on, arrives at her desk and puts her purse down. There's
a* NOTE *on her* CHAIR.

"SAMMY—PLEASE SEE ME."

INT. BANK—HALLWAY. A MOMENT LATER.

TRACKING SAMMY, *coat off, carrying a stack of folders, as she walks
from her desk, around the corner, down the hall, past a couple of employees
and to* BRIAN'S OPEN DOOR. *She taps on it. Brian is at his desk.*

SAMMY

Morning.

BRIAN

Yeah, good morning. Could you get the door?

OUTSIDE THE OFFICE: *Sammy shuts the door.* MABEL *and* DORIS, *standing near the door, look at each other: i.e., Sammy's in trouble again.*

INSIDE THE OFFICE: *Sammy stands by the closed door. Brian comes out around his desk.*

SAMMY

Listen—I just—

Brian kisses her. She drops her folders and they make out against the door.

OUTSIDE THE OFFICE: *The employees click away at their PCs. Mabel exchanges a quiet word with Chuck.*

INSIDE THE OFFICE: *Brian has Sammy pressed against the wall with her skirt hiked up and is trying to get both of their underwear out of the way. It's not so easy in their office clothes. Sammy tears away.*

SAMMY

Brian, that's enough.

BRIAN *falls back, breathless.*

BRIAN

OK. Sorry.

He lunges at her again. They kiss some more.

OUTSIDE THE OFFICE. A MOMENT LATER: *Sammy comes out of the office, more or less composed, carrying her folders. She heads down the hall past the other employees, including Mabel, and surreptitiously readjusts her scrunched-up underwear.*

INT. DAWSON'S. DAY.

Sammy and Bob sit at lunch. Sammy is picking at her food.

> BOB
>
> You're awfully quiet.

> SAMMY
>
> I'm sorry.

> BOB
>
> Um . . . Have you thought at all about what I said?

> SAMMY
>
> Of course I've been thinking about it.

> BOB
>
> So . . . Any decisions? Or—do you still want to think about it some more . . . ?

> SAMMY
>
> Well—I mean—I don't know, Bob. I mean, we haven't exactly been going steady the last few months, if you know what I mean—

> BOB
>
> Yeah, no, I know—

> SAMMY
>
> —and then we see each other twice and you suddenly say you want to get married? I mean . . .

> BOB
>
> No, you're right, you're right—

> SAMMY
>
> What are you *talking* about?

Pause.

> BOB
>
> I don't know . . . I . . . Maybe this is . . . Last year I sort of thought you *were* possibly interested in that . . . idea . . . but I was the one who, you know, wasn't "ready" at that point— So that's why I thought things kind of slowed down with us . . .

> SAMMY
>
> *Don't* make me feel bad for you.

> BOB *(Bristling)*
>
> I don't want you to feel bad for me.

INT. LIVING ROOM. NIGHT.

Sammy, Terry and Rudy are all watching TV. *Sammy and Rudy are in pajamas. Nobody's happy and nobody's talking.*

The PHONE RINGS. *Sammy goes to it and picks up, surprised because of the hour.*

> SAMMY *(Into phone)*
>
> Hello?

> BRIAN *(On phone)*
>
> It's Brian.

Sammy turns away and lowers her voice so Terry and Rudy won't overhear her.

> SAMMY
>
> Brian. Where are you?

EXT. GAS STATION. SIMULTANEOUS.

Brian is on the pay phone outside a gas station.

> BRIAN
>
> I'm buying milk. I just thought I'd say hello.

WE CUT BETWEEN THEM. *Sammy doesn't say anything.*

BRIAN

Look, I know it's probably too late, but is there any way you can come out for a little while?

SAMMY

Brian, I think you're going crazy.

BRIAN

I know I am. Can you meet me?

SAMMY

Um, OK.

INT. LIVING ROOM. NIGHT.

SAMMY *comes down the stairs, fully dressed, into the living room, where Terry and Rudy are still watching* TV.

SAMMY

Um—I have to go out for a minute. Do you want anything?

TERRY

Like what?

SAMMY

I don't know.

RUDY

Where are you going?

TERRY

Yeah, where are you going?

SAMMY

I just have to go out for a little while.

RUDY

Where?

TERRY

Yeah, where?

SAMMY

I just have to go to Mabel's house.

RUDY

Why?

SAMMY

You know what, Rudy? It's personal. This is a personal matter that has to do with Mabel. I just have to go see her for a little while.

Terry gives Sammy a look like, "You've got to be kidding." Sammy tries to shush him with a conspiratorial look back. She goes out.

LATER. *Terry and Rudy sit in front of the TV, alone.*

TERRY

Listen. Listen. I'm sorry I said you squealed on me. I was totally out of line, and I really owe you an apology. *(Pause)* Did you hear what I said?

RUDY *(Staring at the TV)*

I don't care.

INT. SAMMY'S CAR (MOVING). NIGHT.

Sammy drives, listening to music. She shakes her head at herself.

EXT. MOTEL. NIGHT.

Sammy's car and Brian's car are parked side by side outside a roadside motel.

INT. MOTEL ROOM. NIGHT.

In the motel room, Sammy and Brian, half-clothed, make love rather hurriedly on top of the unmade creaky bed.

EXT. MOTEL. NIGHT.

Outside the motel, Sammy and Brian get into their respective cars and start their motors.

INT. SAMMY'S CAR (MOVING). NIGHT.

Sammy drives in the other direction. She breaks into a smile, and then she laughs. Then she stops.

INT. SAMMY'S BEDROOM. NIGHT.

Sammy lies awake plagued by guilty feelings.

EXT. CHURCH—RECTORY. DAY.

Sammy heads toward the little white church building.

INT. CHURCH—RECTORY—OFFICE. DAY.

RON *the* MINISTER *and Sammy drink coffee in silence.*

> RON *(Gently)*
> What's on your mind, Sammy?

> SAMMY
> Well, a lot. But principally . . . I was just wondering if
> you had an opinion. If you know someone, in your
> family, or just someone you really care about, and they
> just can't seem to get ahold of themselves . . .

EXT. MAIN STREET. DAY.

The SUN SHINES *on Main Street.*

INT. SPORTING GOODS STORE. DAY.

*Rudy watches wide-eyed as Terry places on the sales counter two rods
and reels, a bunch of lures, two fishing hats, a box of swivels, a knife
and a fish scaler.*

> TERRY
> You know who this is for?

> RUDY
> Me!

> TERRY
> That's right, my little friend. *(To the saleslady)* Hello.
> We're going fishing.

INT. SAMMY'S HOUSE—KITCHEN. DAY.

*Sammy, Terry and Rudy are all putting away the groceries. Everybody
seems to be getting along.*

> RUDY
> I got a new rod and reel, five lures, I got a hat, I got a
> knife and I got a fish scaler.

                    SAMMY

     That's great, honey.

O.C., *the* DOORBELL RINGS. *Sammy starts to move toward the door,*
but Terry is closer.

                    TERRY

     I'll get it.

Sammy watches him go.

INT./EXT. FRONT DOOR. DAY.

Terry opens the door. It's Ron, the minister, in his civvies.

EXT. FRONT YARD. DAY.

Rudy is playing basketball by himself.

INT. SAMMY'S HOUSE—LIVING ROOM. DAY.

Terry, Sammy and RON *sit in the living room. Sammy and Ron are*
drinking coffee. Through the window we see occasional glimpses of
Rudy playing basketball in the backyard. There is a heavy silence in
the room.

                    TERRY

     Well . . . I'm not really sure why you're here, Ron. I
     mean, I realize I haven't exactly been a model citizen
     since I got here, but compared to how things have been
     goin' for me lately, I thought I was doing pretty well.

He turns to Sammy.

               TERRY *(Cont'd.)*

     And I also find it kind of discouraging that you seem to
     think I need some kind of spiritual counseling or what
     have you, so much so that you're willing to disregard
     the fact that I don't believe in any of this stuff at all—

                    SAMMY

     Well . . . I didn't mean to discourage you—

                    TERRY

     I mean it's really kind of insulting.

RON

Can I say something here? *(Pause)* Sammy asked me to
come and talk to you, because it's her opinion that
you're not gonna find what you're looking for the way
you're looking for it—

TERRY

How would she know?

RON

But I'm really not here to try to get you to do anything,
or to believe anything. And I'll tell you the same thing I
told her, which is that as far as I'm concerned the only
way she can help you is by her example—by trying to be
a model for you, by the way she lives her life . . .

Terry smiles.

RON

And that doesn't mean she's supposed to be a saint,
either, if that's what you're smiling about.

TERRY

I didn't realize I was smiling.

A moment.

RON

You know, Terry, a lot of people come to see me with all
kinds of problems. Drugs, alcohol, marital problems,
sexual problems, health problems—

TERRY

Great job you got.

RON

Well . . . I like it. Because even in this little town, I feel
like what I do is very connected with the real center of
people's lives. I'm not saying I'm always Mr. Effective,
but I *don't* feel like my life is off to the side of what's
important. You know? I *don't* feel my happiness and
comfort are based on closing my eyes to trouble within

myself or trouble in other people. I don't feel like a negligible little scrap, floating around in some kind of empty *void,* with no sense of connectedness to anything around me except by virtue of whatever little philosophies I can scrape together on my own . . .

> TERRY

Well—

> RON

Can I ask you, Terry: Do you think your life is important?

> TERRY

You mean—Like, me personally, my individual life?

> RON

Yeah.

> TERRY

Well . . . I'm not sure— What do you mean? It's important to *me.* I guess. And like, to my, you know, the people who care about me . . .

> RON

But do you think it's *important?*

> TERRY

I—

> RON

Do you think it's important in the *scheme* of things? Not just because it's yours, or because you're somebody's brother. Because I don't really get the impression that you do.

> TERRY

Well, I don't think . . . I don't particularly think *any*body's life has any particular importance besides whatever—you know—whatever we arbitrarily give it. Which is fine. I mean we might as *well* . . . I think I'm as important as anybody *else* . . .

Silence.

TERRY

I don't know: A lot of what you're saying has a real appeal to me, Ron. A lot of the stuff they told us when we were kids. . . . But I don't want to believe something or not believe it because I might feel bad. I want to believe it because I think it's true or not. . . . I'd like to think that my life is important . . . Or that it's connected to something important . . .

RON

Well, isn't there any way for you to believe that without calling it God, or religion, or whatever term it is you object to?

TERRY

Yes. I believe that.

INT. DINING ROOM. NIGHT.

Sammy, Terry and Rudy are all eating dinner. Terry is drinking a beer. His mood is dark.

TERRY

So Sammy, what example will you be setting for us tonight?

Sammy doesn't answer.

INT. LIVING ROOM. NIGHT.

Terry, Sammy and Rudy are watching TV. Terry has another beer.

RUDY

What time are we getting up to go fishing?

TERRY

We're not going fishing.

SAMMY	RUDY
What do you mean?	Why not?

TERRY

I think you should go fishing with Father Ron.

RUDY

I don't want to go fishing with Father Ron.

TERRY

Well, I'm not takin' you.

Sammy starts to say something to Terry, stops herself.

SAMMY

I'll take you, sweetie.

Rudy doesn't answer.

INT. HALLWAY. NIGHT.

Sammy and Terry are in the hallway. Sammy holds a stack of folded sheets.

SAMMY

I realize that you're mad at me—

TERRY *(Deadpan)*

I'm not mad at you . . .

SAMMY

—but he didn't do anything to you. And you cannot promise a little boy that you're gonna—

TERRY *(On "boy")*

. . . I just, you know, after all that religious conversation, I just realized it's probably not so good for him to be spending so much time with someone like me who doesn't believe his life is important in the scheme of things—

SAMMY

Would you please . . .

TERRY

I'm serious.

SAMMY (*Practically choking*)
Listen. (*Pause*) I am sure, if you put your mind to it, you can think of some other way of getting back at me besides this. So would you please just give it some thought, and take him fishing tomorrow?

TERRY
I would, Sammy, I just don't think it'd be good for him.

Pause.

SAMMY
You suck.

She throws the sheets at him and storms away. Terry walks through the living room and OUT *the front door,* SLAMMING *it behind him.*

INT. SAMMY'S ROOM. NIGHT.

Sammy sits by the phone in her bathrobe. She picks it up and DIALS.

INTERCUT: BRIAN'S LIVING ROOM. NANCY, *watching* TV *on the sofa with Brian, picks up the* RINGING PHONE.

NANCY (*Into the phone*)
Hello?

SAMMY HANGS UP. *She gets up, walks around, sits down again. Picks up the phone and* DIALS. *It* RINGS.

INTERCUT: BOB'S KITCHENETTE. *Bob, making a sandwich for himself, picks up the phone.*

BOB (*Into the phone*)
Hello?

SAMMY HANGS UP. *Pause. She sweeps the* TELEPHONE *and* ANSWERING MACHINE OFF *the nightstand. Pause. She calms down and puts them back. The ancient answering machine is* CLICKING *convulsively. She* WHACKS IT *and it stops.*

EXT. CHURCH. DAY.

The congregation is coming out of the church and milling around at the steps. SAMMY, *with Rudy at her side, is saying good-bye to some neighbors. She watches pregnant* NANCY *and* BRIAN *go down the steps.*

POV SAMMY: *Beyond Brian and Nancy,* TERRY *pulls up at the curb in her car. He rummages around and produces* FISHING RODS *which he waves, somewhat sheepishly.*

REVERSE: *At top speed, Rudy runs away from Sammy and the church, toward Terry and the car. Terry and Sammy exchange a look from the distance.*

EXT. RECTORY. DAY.

Services are over. Everyone has gone home.

INT. RON'S OFFICE. LATER.

Sammy sits with Ron.

> SAMMY
> Anyway . . . I don't know what the church's position is on adultery and fornication these days, but I felt really hypocritical not saying anything to you about it before, so . . . What *is* the official position on that stuff these days?

RON

Well . . . it's a sin.

SAMMY

Good: I think it should be.

RON

. . . but we don't tend to focus on that aspect of it, right
off the bat—

SAMMY

Why not?

RON

Well—

SAMMY

I think you should.

RON

Well—

SAMMY

Maybe it was better when you came in and they screamed
at you for having sex with your married boss, and were
really mean to you, and told you what a terrible thing it
was. Maybe it'd be better if you told me how I'm
endangering my immortal soul, and if I don't quit I'm
going to burn in hell. Don't you ever think that?

RON

Um . . . No.

SAMMY

Well, it's a lot better than all this "Why do you think
you're *in* this situation" psychological bullshit you hear
all the time.

RON

Well . . . Why *do* you think you're in this situation?

SAMMY

With which *one*?

All of them.

Pause.

SAMMY

I feel *sorry* for them. *(Pause)* Isn't that ridiculous?

Ron shrugs: i.e., "not necessarily."

EXT. STREAM—BRIDGE. DAY.

Terry and Rudy are side by side on a small footbridge over a wide running stream, fishing. The sunlight slants through the canopy of trees; the birds are chattering; it's gorgeous and peaceful.

RUDY

I've never been so bored in my life.

TERRY

Yeah . . . We really shoulda been out here around seven or eight A.M.

RUDY

What time is it now?

TERRY

Two-thirty.

Silence. The birds sing.

RUDY

Was my father a good fisherman?

TERRY

Yeah, your father was good at all that stuff. He knew everything about the woods, everything about fishing, everything about hunting and everything about cars. If he wasn't such a pain in the ass he would've been a lot of fun to be around.

RUDY

Maybe he's nicer now.

TERRY

I doubt it.

RUDY

Well, I think he is.

TERRY

How would you know? Did you ever meet him?

RUDY

No.

TERRY

Were you ever curious to meet him?

RUDY

I guess so.

TERRY

Well, he doesn't live very far from here.

RUDY

I thought he lived in Alaska.

TERRY

No—*I* lived in Alaska. Your dad lives in Auburn. Far as I know. *(Pause)* We could look him up in the phone book. Wanna try?

RUDY

All right.

TERRY

OK—But— I'm sure I don't have to say this, but I'm
not kidding, man: Don't—tell—your—mother.

INT. BOB'S APARTMENT. DAY.

BOB *is standing by his kitchenette, extremely nervous. Sammy sits on
his sofa.*

BOB

Do you want to go for a walk, or a drive? It's really nice
out.

SAMMY

No. I'm not gonna stay long. Bob, I don't want to get
married.

Pause.

BOB

OK.

SAMMY

I've really thought about it a lot, and if you had asked
me last year I'm sure I would have said yes.

BOB

Oh. Thank you.

SAMMY

But I'm not sure it would have been a good idea then
either. I'm going through a really hard time right now
and I just think that getting engaged to you or anyone
would be just about the stupidest most self-destructive
thing I could possibly do.

BOB

OK.

SAMMY

And I really think you have to grow up.

BOB

Well, how about we fix up my personality some other time?

SAMMY

OK. *(Pause)* I really hope we can still be friends.

BOB *(Quietly sarcastic)*

Oh, yes, me too.

She looks at him miserably.

SAMMY

Bob . . . This is so crazy . . . I mean . . . I don't even understand why you . . . I don't even get it.

BOB

What do you want me to say? Everything you said about me was true, Sammy. I was just a big chickenshit jerk, and now I'm payin' the price.

SAMMY

Bob . . . !

She goes over to him. He gets up.

BOB

What?

SAMMY

Well—I don't know . . .

BOB

I don't know. Sammy, I love you. I wish I could say it in a more interesting way. I just—I love you.

SAMMY

Well—I mean—I love you too—

He puts his arms around her and kisses her. She responds very warmly. Just as things are heating up, she suddenly remembers something and jolts away.

SAMMY

Oh shit.

BOB

What's the matter?

SAMMY

I gotta go. I'm sorry—

BOB

Where do you have to go?

SAMMY (*Off the top of her head*)
I'm supposed to— I gotta get Mabel back her car.

BOB

Well . . . I don't understand. How are we leaving
things?

SAMMY

Oh God, I don't know. Call me later.

INT. MOTEL. DAY.

Brian sits on the edge of one of the beds watching some daytime Sunday show on the motel TV. There is a knock at the door. He gets up, turns off the TV and opens the door. It's Sammy.

SAMMY

Sorry I'm so late.

BRIAN

Yeah, I was just about to give up on you.

SAMMY

Well—maybe it would've been better if you had . . .

She comes into the room and starts walking around briskly and nervously.

SAMMY

I mean— Look, I don't mean to be unsympathetic about
your domestic situation, whatever it is, but I'm just
beginning to think that if people tried a little harder to
stick to their commitments and started taking a little
responsibility for their actions, they might end up
having a lot less trouble generally. That's all.

BRIAN

Hey, that's what I've been trying to tell you guys at the bank.

SAMMY

Well, I really don't think I can do this anymore.

BRIAN

OK.

INT. MOTEL ROOM. LATER.

Brian and Sammy lie under the starchy sheets. Brian's eyes are shut. Sammy is very upset with herself.

SAMMY

This is incredible.

BRIAN

Mmmm.

SAMMY

That is not what I mean.

INT. SAMMY'S CAR (MOVING). DAY.

Terry and Rudy drive along. Terry looks down at Rudy and smiles. Rudy is tense and won't look at him.

OVER TERRY AND RUDY'S SHOULDERS *as Terry drives slowly past dilapidated little houses in a very depressed residential area. Terry is scanning the house numbers.*

RUDY

Maybe we should call first.

TERRY

Well—We're right here.

He pulls up outside a small, plain, run-down ranch-style house with a lot of junk out front, and gets out of the car. Rudy stays in.

TERRY

Come on.

Rudy gets out of the car and comes around. Terry waits for him, and then they walk up to the front door. The buzzer says "KOLINSKI."

TERRY

There he is.

RUDY

His last name is Kolinski?

TERRY

Yeah. Ring the bell.

Rudy pushes the doorbell. They wait. There's some noise inside and some voices. The sound of WALKING.

THE DOOR OPENS. JANIE, *a tired-looking young woman around Terry's age, opens the door.*

JANIE

Yes?

TERRY

Hi. We're looking for Rudy?

JANIE

Who should I say is calling?

TERRY

An old friend.

RUDY SR. *(O.C.)*

Who is it?

JANIE

He says an old friend!

RUDY SR. *(O.C.)*

How old is he?

RUDY SR. *appears behind Janie. He's around thirty, wiry, dressed in jeans and an old shirt. He doesn't look good. He recognizes Terry.*

RUDY SR.

Hey!

TERRY

Hey, Rudy.

Rudy Sr. sees Rudy, who is looking up at him. His face falls.

RUDY SR.

Hey.

Rudy doesn't answer.

TERRY *(To JANIE)*

Hi, I'm Terry.

JANIE

Hello.

TERRY

And this is Rudy.

JANIE

You don't say.

TERRY

Rudy, meet Rudy.

Rudy Sr. looks away, shaking his head. JANIE *moves away from the door.*

JANIE

I'll just be in the kitchen.

TERRY

Nice to meet you.

Janie goes into the kitchen. Rudy Sr. watches her go.

TERRY

OK if we come in for a minute?

RUDY SR.

What the hell are you doin'?

TERRY

What do you mean what am I doin'—

Rudy Sr. starts walking toward Terry to make him go back out the door.

RUDY SR.

Could you step away from the door please?

TERRY

Well we just wanna—

RUDY SR.

Could you step away from the door please?

TERRY

All right, all right.

They all go outside. Rudy Sr. pulls the door closed behind him.

RUDY SR.

What are you doin' here?

TERRY

I just wanted the kid to see you—

RUDY SR.

Well, now he saw me. *(He looks at Rudy)* Now you saw me. OK? *(To Terry)* Now would you mind?

TERRY

Man, you are really—

RUDY SR.

Look: I'm tryin' to be polite. So would you just take off? It's OK: Just take off.

TERRY

I just wanna—

RUDY SR.

Do you know what you're doin'? Just get outta here!

TERRY

You know what, man? You're still a fuckin' asshole.

RUDY SR.

I'm an asshole? Get outta here!

Rudy Sr. shoves Terry. Terry belts him, and suddenly they are throwing wild punches at each other. Rudy goes sprawling in the dirt.

Terry knocks Rudy Sr. down and starts pummeling him brutally. Janie comes out of the house and jumps on his back, trying to pull him off.

> JANIE
> Get your fuckin' hands off him . . . !

Terry throws Janie off him, grabs Rudy Sr. again and resumes beating him up. Janie jumps back on top of him.

Two neighbors run toward the melee to break it up.

CUT TO:

A FEW MOMENTS LATER: *The cops have arrived. The* 1ST COP *is talking to Rudy and Janie. The* 2ND COP *is talking to Terry. Rudy Sr.'s face looks puffy and beaten up. A* 3RD COP *stands apart with Rudy, who is watching the whole thing.* WE CUT *rapidly and jerkily through this section:*

> 1ST COP
> And you're not the boy's legal guardian?

> RUDY SR.
> I don't even know if that's my kid!

> JANIE
> They just showed up! We never seen them before

> RUDY SR.
> I used to know his *sister*—

> TERRY
> I just came down here to talk to the guy and all of a sudden he starts shovin' me!

> 2ND COP
> Listen up. Listen *up.* You're gonna have to step back and just calm down—

> TERRY *(To RUDY SR.)*
> You're a lyin' fuckin' piece of shit.

> 2ND COP *(To TERRY)*
> You're gonna have to step *back.*

> JANIE
> We have a right to protect ourselves. What else do you need to *know*?

A MOMENT LATER: *The* 2ND COP *puts handcuffs on Terry. Rudy watches.*

2ND COP
Now give me your right hand . . .

TERRY	2ND COP
This is such bullshit.	Listen up. Now—
He started the whole	Listen up!
thing and you're	Stop talkin'. Terry,
arresting *me*?	stop talkin'.

CUT TO:

A MOMENT LATER: *As the* 3RD COP *walks Rudy to one cop car, Rudy watches the* 2ND COP *guide the* HANDCUFFED TERRY *into the other car.*

Rudy gets in the back of the car and looks out at RUDY SR. *and* JANIE *talking to the* 1ST COP. *Rudy Sr. is looking at him over the 1st cop's shoulder.*

2ND COP
—idea where we might be able to contact his mother?

RUDY SR.
No, because he's not my Goddamn kid.

The cop cars' doors slam first on Terry and then on Rudy.

INT. MOTEL ROOM. NIGHT.

The room is dark. Sammy and Brian are asleep, half under the covers. SAMMY WAKES *with a* START.

SAMMY
What time is it?

BRIAN *(Startled awake)*
What's the matter?

Sammy looks at the clock radio. 9:20.

SAMMY
Oh my gosh.

A FEW MOMENTS LATER: *Sammy and Brian are on opposite sides of the bed, getting dressed.*

> BRIAN
>
> Hey, you know, Nancy's gonna be gone for the rest of the week . . .

> SAMMY
>
> You know . . . Brian . . .

> BRIAN
>
> Yeah?

> SAMMY
>
> Well, I don't want to . . . I mean, couldn't we just . . . I mean, could we give it a rest?

Pause.

> BRIAN
>
> Um—Yeah. Sure. If you want to.

> SAMMY
>
> I mean . . . I just think . . . I don't know: We had a great little fling. You know? Let's not push it. *(Pause)* I mean, is that OK? I just—

> BRIAN
>
> Yeah. Sure. OK. You're right.

Pause.

> SAMMY
>
> So are we still friends?

> BRIAN *(Nods tersely)*
>
> Mm hm. Sure.

> SAMMY
>
> All right. Good . . . !

EXT. SAMMY'S HOUSE. NIGHT.

The crickets are chattering. The phone is ringing inside the house.

INT. SAMMY'S BEDROOM. SIMULTANEOUS.

The PHONE *is ringing on the* NIGHTSTAND. *The battered answering machine* CLICKS *convulsively but does not pick up.*

INT. SAMMY'S KITCHEN. NIGHT.

Sammy is on the phone in her bathrobe.

> SAMMY
> Around two o'clock this afternoon . . . Yeah, a ninety-three Toyota Tercel. New York plates V127AC . . . Please.

INT. SAMMY'S HOUSE—FRONT DOOR. NIGHT.

Sammy, dressed now, opens the door for BOB. *She is very anxious.*

> SAMMY
> Thanks for coming over. I just want to have a car handy just in case.

> BOB
> No problem.

INT. KITCHEN. NIGHT.

Sammy is on the phone. Bob sits at the table.

> SAMMY *(Into the phone)*
> Well—what about other towns? . . . Yes! Yes! I called the highway patrol *four times*. . . . Well what am I supposed to *do* all night?

INT. SAMMY'S LIVING ROOM. LATER.

Sammy and Bob sit silently in the living room, waiting. She is smoking. The CLOCK READS *12:40. Sammy is going crazy with anxiety.*

EXT. SAMMY'S HOUSE. MORNING.

The PHONE *rings inside the house as the early morning sun slants through the trees around the house.*

INT. LIVING ROOM. SIMULTANEOUS.

The RINGING PHONE *wakes* BOB, *on the sofa in his clothes—*

INT. SAMMY'S BEDROOM. SIMULTANEOUS.

—and Sammy, half asleep on top of her bed, also in her clothes. She GRABS *the* PHONE.

> SAMMY *(Into phone)*
> Hello?

INT. BOB'S CAR (MOVING). DAY.

Bob drives Sammy along the highway. She stares out the window. She turns and watches Bob drive for a long moment.

INT. BANK. DAY.

Brian walks through the morning bank activity and stops at Mabel's desk.

> BRIAN
> Anyone hear from Sammy this morning?

> MABEL
> I didn't.

> BRIAN
> Uh huh. Well, if anyone ever hears from her ever again, will you let me know?

> MABEL
> Yes.

EXT. AUBURN POLICE STATION. DAY.

On the steps of the police station, Sammy, Rudy and Bob wait as Sheriff Darryl shakes hands with the Auburn Sheriff. The Auburn Sheriff goes inside. Darryl comes over to Sammy.

> SHERIFF
> It's gonna be all right. . . . We got on the phone and talked to Rudy Sr. a little bit and he's calmed down, just wants to forget about the whole thing . . .

> SAMMY
> Darryl, I really appreciate this . . .

The Sheriff nods, but he's not thrilled to be here.

INT. SAMMY'S LIVING ROOM. DUSK.

The PHONE IS RINGING. *Sammy comes in the front door, Terry and Rudy behind her. She snaps on the lights, hurries to the phone and picks up.*

Behind her, Rudy goes upstairs and Terry plunks down on the sofa and turns on the TV.

> SAMMY
>
> Hello?

INTERCUT WITH BRIAN, AT THE BANK.

> BRIAN
>
> Yeah, it's Brian.

> SAMMY
>
> Brian—

> BRIAN
>
> What the hell happened to you today, lady?

SAMMY *is about to answer, but she just* HANGS UP *instead.*

BRIAN *is stunned into sheer gaping fury. Feverishly he hangs up and dials again. It* RINGS.

Sammy picks up.

> SAMMY
>
> Hello?

> BRIAN
>
> You're *fired*!

> SAMMY
>
> GOOD!

She hangs up again.

INT. RUDY'S ROOM. NIGHT.

Sammy is tucking Rudy into bed.

SAMMY

Rudy?

RUDY

Yeah?

SAMMY

Is there anything you want to ask me, about your father?

RUDY

Oh, that wasn't my father.

SAMMY

What?

RUDY

That wasn't him. I heard him tell the cops.

SAMMY

No—Rudy—that was him. But that was him. I wish it wasn't, but it was.

RUDY *(Very quiet)*

No it wasn't.

SAMMY

Rudy. Yes it was. Your father's name is Rudy Kolinski. He lives in Auburn . . .

INT. HALLWAY. NIGHT.

Sammy comes out of Rudy's room, shutting the door softly. We HEAR the TV going downstairs. She stands at the top of the stairs for a moment.

INT. LIVING ROOM. NIGHT.

Terry is watching TV on the sofa with his feet up on the coffee table. Sammy comes down the stairs and into the living room. He keeps watching TV. She doesn't sit. She is trembling.

SAMMY

Could you turn that off for a minute please?

He turns off the TV.

> TERRY
>
> You don't have to say anything, Sammy.

> SAMMY
>
> I want you to leave.

Terry looks at her.

> TERRY
>
> What do you mean?

> SAMMY
>
> I mean I don't think you should live here anymore. I don't think you know how to behave around an eight-year-old and I don't know how to make you stop, so I think you shouldn't live here. I don't know what else to say.

> TERRY
>
> I don't know how to behave around an eight-year-old?

> SAMMY
>
> That's right—

> TERRY
>
> I think *you* don't know how to behave around an eight-year-old.

> SAMMY
>
> Are you out of your MIND!?!

Silence.

> SAMMY
>
> Now you just listen to me. I may not be the greatest mother in the world, but I'm doing the best I know how. And he doesn't need you to rub his face in *shit* because you think it's *good* for him. He's going to find out the world is a horrible place and that people *suck* soon enough, and without any help from you. Believe me!

Sammy tries to get ahold of herself. Her voice is shaking.

SAMMY

I think you should get your own place. I thought, if you want, you could— I'll be glad to help you out financially—

TERRY

What do you mean, Get my own place?

SAMMY

I mean I—

TERRY

You mean in Scottsville?

SAMMY

Yes.

TERRY

Why would I do that? Why don't I just leave, period?

SAMMY *(Quietly)*

Well . . . If that's what you want to do, that's fine. But that's not what I'm saying. You are a very important person to Rudy, and you are the *most* important person to me. But I'm saying that I can't take any more of this—

TERRY

Well—

SAMMY

—I thought—maybe you could sell your half of the house to me, and I could pay you whatever it is over a certain amount of time, and that way—

TERRY

No, you know what? I'll just go.

He turns the TV *back on.*

SAMMY *(Very quietly)*

Well—that's not what I'm saying.

Terry shrugs and watches TV.

INT. TERRY'S ROOM. NIGHT.

Terry is packing his bag. Rudy is watching.

RUDY

Where are you going?

TERRY

I don't know. I just want to get out of this town. And
if you've got any sense when you get old enough you'll
get out of here too. Your Mom's gonna live in this
town for the rest of her life, and you know why?
Because she thinks she has to. Don't ask me why, but
that's the truth. She thinks there's all these things she
has to do, but you want to know one thing about your
Mom? She's a bigger fuck-up than I ever was. I mean,
I know I messed up. You think I enjoy getting thrown
in *jail* because I wanted you to face that prick your
Dad like a little man and see what kind of a guy he is?
I know I got a little carried away, and I lost my
temper just a little bit—which is not the end of the
world either, by the way, just for future reference—
And now she's kickin' me out of my own house
because—you know, because I fucked up a little bit.
Which I totally admit. I was like—totally ready to
admit that.

He is finished stuffing his clothes into his backpack.

RUDY

I could go with you.

TERRY

Well, thanks, man. But I, uh, I can't really take care of
you.

INT. LIVING ROOM. NIGHT.

*Sammy is flipping channels on the TV. The DOORBELL RINGS. She is
surprised. She gets up. Terry comes thundering down the stairs, carrying his backpack.*

SAMMY

Is that for you?

TERRY

Yeah, I'm just gonna stay at Ray's till I take off.

SAMMY

You don't have to do that.

TERRY

Yeah. Well, that's what I wanna do, so—

SAMMY

Well but— Are you gonna come back to say good-bye?

TERRY

No—I'm just gonna take off. I'll see you later.

SAMMY

Well—

Terry opens the door. RAY *is there. Terry closes the door behind him. Sammy listens to the* PICKUP TRUCK DRIVE OFF. *The sound* FADES.

INT. RAY'S HOUSE. NIGHT.

Terry is bunked down on Ray's horrible sofa. In the b.g., there is a light on in the bedroom. Terry fluffs his pillow and shuts his eyes.

EXT. SAMMY'S HOUSE. DAY.

Dressed for work and school, Sammy and Rudy walk to the car.

SAMMY

Look. I know you're upset about Uncle Terry leaving, and so am I. But he's just not in control of himself, and I don't want him hurting your feelings anymore—or mine. And you may not like it, but that's how it's gotta be. OK?

RUDY

I don't care.

SAMMY

You don't care. I don't care either.

INT. BRIAN'S OFFICE. DAY.

Sammy sits in front of Brian's desk.

> BRIAN
>
> Well . . . I'm sorry you're havin' all this trouble . . .

> SAMMY
>
> Thank you.

> BRIAN
>
> But you made a pretty good speech to me yesterday about people sticking to their commitments . . .

> SAMMY
>
> Yeah . . . ?

> BRIAN
>
> Well . . . you made a commitment to this bank, Sammy. To this job.

> SAMMY
>
> I know I d——

> BRIAN
>
> And to working things out with this tough new son of a bitch boss of yours. And whatever might have passed between us after hours doesn't mean you just walk away from that commitment—yeah, even when you have a legitimate family emergency.

> SAMMY
>
> I'm really sorry I didn't—

> BRIAN
>
> Which is why I think in the calm cold light of day, we should both think real hard about whether or not you really want to continue on here at Merchants National Trust.

> SAMMY
>
> You're not serious.

BRIAN

. . . you're not happy, I'm not happy, it's not good for you and it sure as heck isn't good for the bank.

Pause.

SAMMY

You know you're the worst manager we've ever had?

BRIAN

Come on, Sammy . . .

SAMMY

By *far* the worst.

BRIAN

. . . I don't wanna trade insults with you.

SAMMY

Well, I don't want to be fired, Brian. I've been working here for seven years.

BRIAN

Well—

SAMMY

And if I were you I'd be a little nervous about firing an employee I just had an affair with. OK?

BRIAN

That's—Don't threaten me, Sammy: *I'm* not threatening *you.* I—It's just an area I think we should explore.

SAMMY

I'm not thr——

SAMMY

You explore it. I'm going back to work.

She heads for the door, stops.

SAMMY

Oh, and I have to pick up Rudy today because there's no one else to do it. But I'll find someone as soon as I have time.

BRIAN

Yeah. Fine. Why don't you just take over the whole
bank?

*Sammy hesitates in the doorway. This thought has never occurred to her
before. She goes out.*

INT. LUNCH PLACE. DAY.

THROUGH THE WINDOW *we see Sammy and Bob having lunch.
Sammy watches him eat, full of mixed feelings about him.*

INT. KITCHEN. DAY.

*Sammy is at the stove, making pancakes. She puts a last pancake onto
Rudy's plate and brings it to him.*

SAMMY

Well, I called where Uncle Terry said he was gonna stay,
and there was no answer, so I don't know if he's still in
town or not.

Rudy doesn't answer.

SAMMY

Rudy? Are you not speaking to me?

Rudy doesn't answer.

SAMMY

Well, I'm sorry you're so mad at me, but I only did what
I thought I had to do, and I hope you don't stay mad at
me for the rest of your life.

He opens the maple syrup and pours it on the pancakes.

SAMMY

Rudy, that's too much.

*He keeps pouring. She grabs the bottle from him and upsets some of the
dishes on the table.*

SAMMY

You gotta cut this out!

RUDY

What did I do?

SAMMY

You don't know what you're talking about! There was
nothing else I could do! I can't explain it better than that,
but you can't go on like this because you don't know
anything about it and you don't know what you're doing!

RUDY *(Frightened)*

OK, I'm sorry!

SAMMY

I don't want you to be sorry, I just want you to STOP
IT!

RUDY

I will! I will! I'm stopping, I'm sorry.

He comes around the table to her.

RUDY

See? I'm stopping! I'm not doing it. See? I'm not.

He's very alarmed. Sammy looks at him for a long moment.

EXT. CEMETERY. DAY.

*Terry walks through the little cemetery gate and makes his way up the
hill through the tombstones. He reaches his parents' graves. He looks at
the tombstones for a moment. He puts his hand on top of one headstone,
then the other.*

He sits down and smokes. He looks up at the SKY. *It's a beautiful deep
blue sky dotted with billowy white clouds.*

*He looks out over the hilly scenery. After a moment he shakes his head
a few times. He doesn't even know he's doing it. He sits there.*

INT. RAY'S HOUSE. DAY.

The PHONE IS RINGING *as Terry walks into the house. He walks past
it, to the fridge, gets a beer and opens it. It* KEEPS RINGING. *He picks
it up.*

TERRY *(Into phone)*

Ray's house.

INT. BANK—SAMMY'S DESK. DAY.

Sammy is at her desk on the phone.

SAMMY

Hi.

WE CUT BETWEEN THEM. *Terry doesn't say anything.*

SAMMY

I didn't know if you left yet.

TERRY

No—I'm leavin' tomorrow.

SAMMY

Well—What time?

TERRY

There's a bus at nine.

SAMMY

Well—Can I—I'd like to see you before you go. I mean, can I give you a lift? Or do you want to have breakfast or anything? And I think Rudy would really like to say good-bye.

TERRY

Yeah—I don't know . . . I mean—

SAMMY

Terry, you can't just *leave* like this. I—

TERRY

All right, all right. I'll come by in the morning.

SAMMY

All right— But just— We have to be out of the house by eight, so— I don't want to tell Rudy you're coming unless you really think you can make it—

TERRY

Yeah— No— I'll be there.

All right.

SAMMY
TERRY

All right.

INT. KITCHEN. MORNING.

Sammy is clearing the breakfast dishes. Rudy is finishing up his cereal. The clock reads 7:50.

SAMMY

You should get your sneakers on.

EXT. HOUSE. A MOMENT LATER.

Sammy comes out and looks up and down the road.

INT. LIVING ROOM. A FEW MOMENTS LATER.

Rudy sits in the living room in his baseball jacket. His knapsack is on the floor beside him. He looks at the CLOCK: 8:06. *Sammy comes into the living room and looks at him.*

SAMMY

Sweetie, I'm sorry, we have to go.

RUDY

Why can't I miss school one day?

They HEAR *the* PICKUP PULL UP OUTSIDE, O.C. *Rudy gets up immediately.*

EXT. THE HOUSE. A MOMENT LATER.

Terry jumps out of RAY'S PICKUP. *Sammy opens the front door and Rudy runs out toward Terry.*

RUDY

Hi!

TERRY

Hey, how's it goin', man?

Rudy stops short in front of Terry. Terry looks at Sammy, in the door-way.

Sorry I'm late.

EXT./INT. CAR. DAY.

The car stops across the street from the BUS. *The* LAST KIDS *are getting in.* SAMMY HONKS *for the bus driver, and Sammy, Terry and Rudy all get out.*

TERRY

So Rudy . . . If I write you a letter, will you write me back?

RUDY

Yeah.

TERRY

OK, well, that's gonna be pretty nice for you, because I write a pretty Goddamn interesting letter.

RUDY

Yeah, we'll see.

TERRY

All right. Well, say good-bye.

RUDY

Bye.

Rudy hugs Terry. Terry hugs him back. He is suddenly overcome and presses his lips to the top of Rudy's head.

Rudy walks to the BUS *and gets on. The bus pulls away.*

Alone now, Sammy and Terry are not that comfortable. He moves to get back in the car, and she does the same.

EXT. BENCH. DAY.

Sammy and Terry sit on a bench near the bus stop. Terry's backpack is by his side.

SAMMY

Do you need some cash for the bus?

TERRY

No, I got a few bucks. . . . Aren't you gonna be late for work?

SAMMY

Oh—Yeah. That's OK. *(Pause)* Terry, I don't even know where you're going.

TERRY

Oh, well, I didn't really have a concrete plan yet. I have to go back to Worcester and get my stuff . . .

SAMMY

Oh, are you gonna try to see that girl?

TERRY

Well . . . Yeah . . . You know . . . Thought maybe I'd try to show my face . . . Let her brother have a crack at me . . .

SAMMY

What?

TERRY

No . . .

SAMMY

. . . I don't want anyone to have a crack at you.

TERRY

I'm just kidding. I just thought . . . Just thought I'd
check up on her . . . *(Pause)* Anyway, after that, I don't
really know. I've been thinking about Alaska a lot. I still
got some friends out there. I don't really know. Anyway,
I'll write you.

SAMMY

You will?

TERRY

Sure, Sammy. Of course I will. You know that.

Pause.

SAMMY

What is gonna happen to you?

TERRY

Nothing too bad . . . But I gotta tell you, I know things
didn't work out too well this time . . .

SAMMY

Well, Terry—

TERRY

. . . but it's always really good to know that wherever I
am, whatever stupid shit I'm doing, you're back at my
home, rooting for me.

SAMMY

I do root for you.

She starts crying, and looks down.

TERRY

Come on, Sammy. Everything's gonna be all right. . . .
Comparatively . . . And I'll be back this way . . .

SAMMY

I feel like I'm never gonna see you again . . . !

TERRY

Of course you will, Sammy. You never have to worry about that.

SAMMY

Please don't go till you know where you're going. Please . . . !

TERRY

I do know where I'm going. I'm going to Worcester and I'm gonna try to see that girl. And then depending on what happens there, I thought I'd try to see if there's any work for me out West. And if there is, I'm gonna head out there for the summer and try to make some money. And if there isn't, I'll figure something else out. Maybe I'll stay around the East. I don't know . . . I really liked it in Alaska. It was really beautiful. You just— It made me feel good. And before things got so messed up I was doin' pretty well out there. Seriously. But I couldn't stay here long, Sammy: I don't want to live here. But I'm gonna stay in touch. And I'll be back. 'Cause I want to see you and I want to see Rudy. I'll come home for Christmas. How about that? We'll have Christmas together. *(Pause)* Come on, Sammy. You can trust me . . .

Still looking down, Sammy shakes her head, tears leaking down her cheeks.

TERRY

Come on, Sammy . . . Look at me . . . Look at me . . .

She looks at him.

TERRY

Hey, Sammy . . . Remember when we were kids, remember what we always used to say to each other . . . ? *(Pause)* Remember when we were kids?

SAMMY

Of course I do . . . !

She throws her arms around his neck. He pats her gently.

INT./EXT. BUS. DAY.

The DOORS OPEN *and Terry comes up the steps and into the bus. Outside, Sammy watches him pay the driver and move through the bus toward his seat. The* BUS DOORS CLOSE.

EXT. BUS. CONTINUOUS.

Sammy waves till the BUS DRIVES *all the way down* MAIN STREET, *turns a corner and is gone.*

INT. BUS. CONTINUOUS.

Terry, in his seat, turns forward and watches the view go by. He smiles a little.

INT. SAMMY'S CAR (MOVING). DAY.

The morning sunlight flickers through the windshield into the car as Sammy drives along toward work. She passes the TOWN HALL CLOCK *and sees that it's 9:20.*

She dries her damp cheek with a forearm and rolls down her window to let the morning breeze blow through.

Squaring her shoulders a little, she drives through town at a slow and easy pace.

THE END

CREDITS